THE BUZZ

ABOUT THIS BOOK AND ITS AUTHOR

I am impressed with LaMar Boschman's heart for
God and his heart to help people encounter God.
ROBERT MORRIS

This book is a must have for every person seeking
more of God and to be closer to Him.
CHRISTINE D'CLARIO

Encounter implies a moment in time when
something stand before us and our focus
shifts...In the pages ahead, I challenge you to
go deeper than you have ever gone before.
JENTEZEN FRANKLIN

In these pages you will not only find marvelously
written recounts of Biblical encounters with God's
manifested presence, but you will also find it to be
a guide that helps ignite your heart...to passionately
pursue a loving God who, more than anything, wants
your fellowship and to bless you beyond measure.

CHRISTINE D'CLARIO

FOREWORD BY JENTEZEN FRANKLIN

ENCOUNTER

PASSIONATELY PURSUING
GOD'S MANIFEST PRESENCE

LAMAR BOSCHMAN

ENCOUNTER

ISBN (print): 978-0998054544

Unless otherwise noted, all Scripture quotations are from the New King James Version of the Bible. Copyright © 1979, 1980, 1982 by Thomas Nelson Inc. publishers. Used by permission.

Scripture quotations marked AMP are from the Amplified Bible. Old Testament copyright © 1965, 1987 by the Zondervan Corporation.

The Amplified New Testament copyright © 1954, 1958, 1987 by the Lockman Foundation. Used by permission..

Scripture quotations marked NAS are from the New American Standard Bible. Copyright © 1960, 1962, 1963, 1968, 1971, 1972, 1973, 1975, 1977 by the Lockman Foundation. Used by permission.

Scripture quotations marked NEB are from the New English Bible. Copyright © 1961, 1970 by the Delegates of the Oxford University Press and the Syndics of the Cambridge University Press. Used by permission.

Scripture quotations marked NIV are from the Holy Bible, New International Version. Copyright © 1973, 1978, 1984, International Bible Society. Used by permission.

Scripture quotations marked RSV are from the Revised Standard Version of the Bible. Copyright © 1946, 1952, 1971 by the Division of Christian Education of the National Council of the Churches of Christ in the USA. Used by permission.

LAMARBOSCHMAN.COM PUBLISHERS

DEDICATION

This book is dedicated to the unknown and unsung musicians and ministers, prophets and pastors who pioneered the biblical truth that God dwells in the singing prayers and praise of His people. I know, because I have heard their stories and the price they paid of ridicule, rebuke, and expulsion for believing God's word for what it says,

> But You are holy, Enthroned in the praises of Israel.
> Psalms 22:3 NKJ

To those men and women, we owe you our gratitude for believing and teaching this profound and powerful truth. For in it is the secret to enter God's revealed presence and encounter His manifested power. It is on your shoulders we stand today--a new generation that does not know that this recent truth was revealed in 1948.

We are grateful and appreciative of your sacrifice and determination to see future generations encounter the revealed presence of a Holy God who invites us to come close.

PREFACE

The presence of God can be both a very comforting and a very terrible force. It can be a sanctuary of intimate communion, bringing a sense of great peace and comfort. At the same time, it can exert a force that actually slays multitudes. On occasion, in Biblical times, the presence of the Lord destroyed entire armies, caused large numbers of men to go blind and whole nations to become ill.

On one such occasion, an entire Assyrian army of one hundred and eighty-five thousand men was destroyed in one night, as God moved by His awesome presence among them. The next morning, only corpses remained. The presence of God killed Egyptian and Hebrew first-bom one unforgettable gloomy night in Egypt. Only those who had blood sprinkled on their door posts escaped.

The Bible says:

> ...as wax melts in front of the fire, so do the
> wicked perish in God's presence. But the
> righteous are glad and rejoice in his presence;
> they are happy and shout for joy.
> Psalms 68:2-3 GNT

What a difference there is in the effect God's presence has on people! In some, it causes great joy, while — in others — it causes great sorrow. There is a direct connection between the relationship people have with the Lord and how His presence affects them.

God's presence can bring terror to those who do not love and serve Him. To those of us who do love Him, He calls— to come into His manifest presence joyfully and expectantly.

God's presence, how we enter, and what happens when we come into His presence are the subjects of this book, one that I believe will change your life forever. Through it, you can learn to know God's presence in your daily life—in your home, in your school or in your office—not just in your church building. In these pages, we will learn how to enter into God's revealed presence at any time and in any place. And learning the secrets of entering God's presence anywhere and at any time will speed us on our way toward our ultimate goal as believers—living in His presence.

LAMAR BOSCHMAN

TABLE OF CONTENTS

FOREWORD BY
xiii **JENTEZEN FRANKLIN**

xv INTRODUCTION
FROM THE AUTHOR

SECTION ONE
OMNI
3 CHAPTER ONE
PARADISE
15 CHAPTER TWO
PLAN

SECTION TWO
EVERYWHERE
25 CHAPTER THREE
BOUNDLESS
33 CHAPTER FOUR
PRESENT
41 CHAPTER FIVE
UNCHANGING

SECTION THREE
MANIFEST

53   CHAPTER SIX
REVEALED

61   CHAPTER SEVEN
APPEARANCES

69   CHAPTER EIGHT
MANIFESTATIONS

79   CHAPTER NINE
ARK

89   CHAPTER TEN
GLORY

101   CHAPTER ELEVEN
THEOPHANY

113   CHAPTER TWELVE
LORD OF ARMIES

121   CHAPTER THIRTEEN
PRESENCES

131   CHAPTER FOURTEEN
IMMANUEL

137   CHAPTER FIFTEEN
PROMISE

SECTION FOUR
ENCOUNTERS

149   CHAPTER SIXTEEN
ENOCH

155   CHAPTER SEVENTEEN
ABRAHAM

165   CHAPTER EIGHTEEN
JACOB

173   CHAPTER NINETEEN
MOSES

183   CHAPTER TWENTY
DAVID

191   CHAPTER TWENTY-ONE
OBED-EDOM

199   CHAPTER TWENTY-TWO
SATAN

207   CHAPTER TWENTY-THREE
HIS PERSON

SECTION FIVE
MANIFEST

217   CHAPTER TWENTY-FOUR
DARKNESS

225   CHAPTER TWENTY-FIVE

UNBELIEVER

233   CHAPTER TWENTY-SIX

BELIEVER

SECTION SIX
PURSUIT

243   CHAPTER TWENTY-SEVEN

PRIVILEGE

251   CHAPTER TWENTY-EIGHT

PORTALS

261   CHAPTER TWENTY-NINE

SEEK

271   CHAPTER THIRTY

CHALLENGE

279   MEET THE AUTHOR

FOREWORD

Jentezen Franklin

ENCOUNTER. What a powerful word. It implies a moment in time when something stands before us and our focus shifts. In that moment we do more than merely notice, we experience something extraordinary and memorable.

True worship, in its purest form, always finds us at the foot of the cross in awe and wonder, not just at what God has done, but because of the indescribable filling and presence of the Holy Spirit. It's in those moments that you know beyond a shadow of a doubt that God is real, and that He knows who you are.

Only gratitude and surrender can also occupy these moments, knowing we are marked for something bigger than ourselves by the God of the universe, that goes beyond "encounter" into what LaMar refers to in this book, "The Manifest Presence of God."

There are dimensions of our glorious King that will never be revealed to the casual, disinterested worshiper. There are walls of intercession what will never be scaled by dispassionate religious service. But when you take steps to break out of the ordinary and worship Him, as He deserves, you will begin to see facets of His being you never knew existed. He will begin to share secrets with you about Himself, His plans, and His desires for you. When you worship God as He deserves, He is magnified.

In the pages ahead, I challenge you to go deeper than you have ever gone before. God is calling you higher and every next step of promotion begins in humble, public and private moments of worship and by pausing to remember and testify to God's faithfulness through praise.

INTRODUCTION

The phrase "the presence of God" is commonly used today and yet so many Christians and even church leaders do not know what the presence of God is and how to explain it to those that want to know.

Some think the presence of God is a feeling or some state they find themselves in while singing their favorite worship songs.

I wrote this book for two reasons. One to explain what the omnipresence of God is and what His manifest presence is. It is important to know the distinctions in order to have a correct perspective of God's presence. Also this understanding leads us into the experience of the true revelation of what His manifest presence is.

The second reason I wrote this book is to point the way to God's manifest presence so that hungry hearts can encounter Him.

I just received this email today from a follower of Jesus that is so desperate to know Him more. It reads...

"Would you pray for me? I need a deep encounter with Jesus! All in me longs SO MUCH for Him!! For DEEP intimacy with Him!

I really have to KNOW our Father and His love for me! I need His healing for my broken heart and my wounded spirit.

I need His breakthrough!! His supernatural intervention!

I want to give everything for Jesus and His kingdom! All for His glory. I want to run BOLDLY for Him! I need His fire!!"

It is for believers and leaders desperate for God, like this woman, who want more of God and the power of His presence in their lives that I pour my heart out in these pages.

Do you have a passion for His presence? Many men in the Bible who experienced God's presence had a strong desire to not only encounter God but to remain there. They are an example to us.

In the following pages you will discover what the presence of God is, how to enter God's manifest presence, and how to develop a desire to live there.

One thing I have asked of the
Lord, and that I will seek:
That I may dwell in the house of the Lord
[in His presence] all the days of my life,
To gaze upon the beauty [the delightful
loveliness and majestic grandeur] of the Lord
And to meditate in His temple.

For in the day of trouble He will
hide me in His shelter;
In the secret place of His tent He will hide me;
He will lift me up on a rock.
And now my head will be lifted up
above my enemies around me,
In His tent I will offer sacrifices with shouts of joy;
I will sing, yes, I will sing praises to the Lord.
Ps 27:4-6 AMP

I desire that David's prayer would be your prayer as you read this book. Prayerfully take in every chapter and answer the questions that will prompt your spirit to blaze with a passion to encounter Him no matter the cost.

OMNI

○————————————————————————————————○

You aren't a waste of space or of God's time.
He created you for a purpose. Draw near
to Him and let Him speak to you!
- Kari Jobe

1

PARADISE

○──○

The numinous power bent down into the lower world He had designed and reached deep into the dirt. Grabbing a handful of red soil and rolling it between His thumb and forefinger He formed a clay figure. Then He bent down lower and blew into the figurine, and it instantly became a living soul.

The Designer looked at His clay creature and affectionately smiled and named him "red one," or Adam. Then He placed His living sculpture in a very prestigious and precious place called paradise.

EDEN

> Now the Lord God had planted a garden in the east,
> in Eden, and there He put the man He had formed.
> Genesis 2:8 NTV

The Progenitor and Creator manifested His presence by lovingly preparing a paradise and placing Adam in it. Eden was not only an emblem of His love, but also a result of His presence. As a hen patiently and carefully prepares a nest for its chicks, Father formed a special place for His creature to dwell in abundance and safety.

THE PROGENITOR MANIFESTED HIS PRESENCE BY LOVINGLY PREPARING A PARADISE

First, God's potent presence created the oasis, and then it created the man.

In a remarkable exercise of power, God manifested His presence a third time by personally doing surgery on the man, removing his rib, designing a woman from it, and placing her by Adam's side.

> So the Lord God caused the man to fall into a deep
> sleep, and while he was sleeping, he took one of the
> man's ribs and closed up the place with flesh. Then the
> Lord God made a woman from the rib he had taken
> out of the man, and he brought her to the man.
> Genesis 2:21-22 NIV

There now existed a divinely matched couple perfectly formed in the paradise of God's presence. It was a glorious display and demonstration of God's affection and love. He had wanted creatures to commune with. There they were.

Adam and Eve lived in an ideal setting. They had everything they needed. They were safe and had nothing to worry about. Life for them was not a daily struggle for existence but a joyful walk with God and with each other. They were "set for life" in paradise. God's presence and man's existence were inseparable.

ENTICED

It wasn't long afterwards that the dragon-lizard saw the couple and desired to deceive them. It bothered the dragon that they were enjoying the spot and receiving such favor when they were so inferior to him.

"There they are—God's little darlings!" the dragon smirked with evil in his eyes.

The dragon-lizard ducked behind a large floral plant not wanting to be seen. He often moved in stealth. The leaves were huge and lush—a perfect hiding place from the eyes of those he wanted to destroy.

The dragon had been watching the couple for a while, observing their movements and listening to their conversations.

The clay couple enjoyed the favor and blessings of God's lush oasis. They explored everything about the oasis—the plants, insects, birds, animals, and the flowers as well as the fruit.

Each day toward dusk God would reveal Himself to the clay couple, and together they would walk through the oasis and converse. The newly created mortals had so many questions.

The couples infatuation and fascination with their Father angered the dragon-lizard because he once was in a similar spot. It was a celestial spot before the throne of God. As the mighty musical cherub, he had covered the manifest presence of God with celestial adoration. He was next to the throne—the center of heaven's attention—until his demotion and eviction from the presence.

The dragon was very crafty and cunning. He would not rest from trying to destroy Adam and Eve and devised a scheme to make them lose confidence in God's Word and disobey and disappoint Him. He was going to destroy the darling couple.

On this day, he perched on a rock and called out to the humans.

"Hey there! I see you enjoy this plush paradise."

"Yes," the woman said, "We enjoy it very much! It is so satisfying to explore its beauty and eat its fruit. It is all very tasty!" Then she paused.

"However, we can't eat all of the fruit."

"Have you tried those?" pointing to the fruit of the tree of the knowledge of good and evil.

"No, God told us we are not to eat of that one! If we did we would die!"

"You won't die!" the dragon insisted. "In fact, God knows that in the day you eat of it your eyes will be opened, and you will be like God, knowing good and evil."

The dragon knew that if he could entice man to go against God's express commands, he could break the bond of fellowship that existed between them. He challenged what God had said by twisting the truth.

Despite the fact that the dragon-lizard was directly contradicting God, he did it in such a manner that it sounded reasonable, seducing Eve by his words. She had not yet learned that fellowship with the Lord demands a quick and cheerful response to His voice.

The dragon's words appealed to Eve. She wanted to ascend in ability and power and have the knowledge of good and evil, so she ate the forbidden fruit. At that moment, she,—the lives of the entire human race, both physically and spiritually—were transformed.

The notion to be like God appealed to the woman, and, besides, she was curious how the fruit tasted. She impulsively reached out and plucked the fruit and examined it.

"Go ahead try it! It's good!" The dragon insisted.

When the woman saw that the tree was good for food, pleasant to the eyes, and desirable to make one wise, she took a bite and gave it to her man.

"Here, try this Adam! It is wonderful!"

Adam took the brightly colored fruit from Eve's hand. He inspected it, smiled, and then bit into it. The succulent juices ran down his chin and onto his chest.

"Mm, this is good!" Adam mumbled with his mouth full.

At that moment they heard God coming their way.

"Eve, quick let's hide!" Adam loudly whispered.

> Then the man and his wife heard the sound of the Lord
> God as He was walking in the garden in the cool of the
> day, and they hid from the Lord God among the trees
> of the garden. But the Lord God called to the man,
> "Where are you?" He answered, "I heard you in the
> garden, and I was afraid because I was naked. So I hid."
> Genesis 3:8-10 NIV

God's footsteps thundered in their ears as He approached. Then they heard His comforting voice gliding on the evening breeze. He was calling them. But this time something seemed to be different to them about His voice. It was no longer comforting; it was terrifying. They crouched in the shadows, hoping that He would not detect them and would go away and leave them alone.

HEARD THE SOUND OF GOD AS HE WAS WALKING IN THE GARDEN

"Where are you?" God inquired though He knew exactly where they were.

God and Adam had begun a custom of walking and talking together. Each looked forward to these moments of intimate communion. Adam had always embraced God's presence and enjoyed their times together. Uncharacteristically the couple turned and hid behind the trees.

Adam and Eve's absence was a clear indication that something was terribly wrong. They acted out of character, hiding from Him in shame.

God made a sound as He walked in the garden, and Adam and Eve knew the sound of God's approach.

The sound had always reminded them of their Creator, of the One who loved them and kept them, who taught them, who answered their every question and every need. He was everything to them.

What God was really asking is, "Why are you hiding?"

God hadn't come to visit them to condemn Adam and Eve. He came, as always, to have fellowship with them. Surely, if they had repented of their wrong and asked His forgiveness, it would have been readily granted.

God wanted Adam to tell Him why he was not running to meet Him as he normally did. He wanted him to admit why he was not eager to see Him, why he was hiding.

God's question was an invitation to confess or repent for what Adam had done. However, Adam was not willing to tell God that he had failed.

FAILURE

This time, when Adam and Eve heard the sound of God walking in the garden, they were not pleased—but frightened. They knew they had let Him down.

Adam replied: "I heard Your voice. …I was afraid because I was naked, and I hid myself."

Adam was now self-conscious, concerned with how he looked in the presence of God. That hadn't concerned him before. Sin makes you uncomfortable in the presence of God; it makes you self-conscience instead of God-conscience.

Adam attributed his fear to the state of his flesh. He was more conscious of the effects of his sin than of the sin itself. Sin confuses people. Not only does it deceive us and rob us of God's presence, but also it brings confusion.

Sin changed everything. After the man and the women realized that they had sinned, the thought of encountering God was no longer a pleasant one. Sin destroyed man's delight and desire to encounter God. They were now afraid of His manifest presence and dreaded His coming. Disobedience to God and His Word becomes a barrier to fellowship with Him.

CURSES

In the aftermath of the fall, more damage was done to the relationship. The result of the fall was a curse upon Adam, a curse upon Eve, and a curse upon the serpent. The greatest part of the curse, for humanity and it's parents, was the banishment from the presence of God.

> God: "Look, the human has now become like one of
> Us...." So the Eternal God banished Adam and Eve from
> the Garden of Eden and exiled humanity from paradise."
> Genesis 3:22-24 Voice

Adam and Eve could no longer walk and talk with their Creator.

Although this part of the curse was directed to the man, it seems clear that the woman was also banished from the garden, as well as the serpent. From that day on, the serpent would crawl on his belly like a snake and eat the dust of the earth.

This is a lesson to us. Don't hide yourself from God's presence for any reason. He wants you to draw near His revealed presence. Come boldly to God's presence. Grace and forgiveness are there. If there is sin in your heart, confess it to the Lord, turn from it.

EXILED

The result of Adam and Eve's failure was not only life changing but history changing.

> The Lord God sent Adam away from the Garden of
> Eden, to till and cultivate the ground from which he
> was taken. So God drove the man out, and at the east
> of the Garden of Eden He [permanently] stationed the
> cherubim and the sword with the flashing blade which
> turned round and round [in every direction] to protect
> and guard the way (entrance, access) to the tree of life.
> Genesis 3:23-24 AMP

As the result of their disobedience, Adam and Eve were expelled from the paradise they had enjoyed so much. Dejected and rejected, they became vagabonds and nomads, drifting from place to place, trying to scrape together an existence by toiling in the dirt.

THE GREATEST PART OF THE CURSE WAS THE BANISHMENT FROM THE PRESENCE OF GOD

The man and woman were exiled from the place for which they were designed—the manifest presence of God. Like fish out of water, they gasped for life and grasped for provision. Humanity was not made to live outside the manifest presence of God.

This was far less than what God had intended for them. Adam and Eve had rejected God's presence and suffered the consequences. Death and decay began their work in their minds and bodies. Humanity would be permanently altered.

SCHEME

What a shock it must have been for Adam and Eve when they found themselves locked out of the garden and deprived of the blessings of God for their lives! They had never known what it was like to be without God's presence. Now, not only had their lives been turned upside down but also there was another presence in their lives—an evil one.

This new presence—dark and deliberate—constantly competed for their attention and separated them from the Lord and His presence. The Serpent will do anything to get between man and God.

The tactic of the Serpent was to get Adam's and Eve's eyes off the Lord and set them on being god-like and having knowledge and power. They reached for something that was not to be theirs. They focused on themselves—on self-gratification, self-fulfillment, selfishness and self-seeking. Anytime we ascend out of our appointment and God's will for us and put our own interests above the Lord, we are in jeopardy of losing the presence of God. The moment we become self-seeking, sin will shortly follow and will alienate us from God's precious presence.

The sin of disobedience had done its horrendous work. No longer did the presence of the Lord cover Adam's and Eve's lives and warm their hearts with the sense of His nearness.

ABNORMAL

For the first time, the man and the woman felt shame and fear—the fear of God and His presence. What had been to them, until that day, cause for rejoicing now became cause for alarm.

LIKE A FISH OUT OF WATER, THEY GASPED FOR LIFE AND GRASPED FOR PROVISION

What a horrible thing it was for them to be alienated from the Lord! They had been the most intimate of friends with Him.

Adam and Eve were caught in a trap with no way of escape. Sin isolated them from Father, and they saw no way to get back to Him. They knew nothing yet of God's Lamb, sacrificed to take their place.

God felt the loss of Adam and Eve's fellowship as much as Adam and Eve felt the loss of God's provision. God wanted friends—companions.

Justice demanded that Adam leave the garden God had prepared for him. Adam had to begin to earn his own way by plowing and planting in soil that was cursed. That day the curse came upon man, upon woman, upon the beasts, and upon the land.

FUGITIVE

The greatest result of Adam's sin was separation from God's presence. Intimacy and fellowship with the Divine was seemingly forever broken. The barrenness of man's new surroundings spoke of the barrenness of his relationship with his Creator, a relationship that was once as fertile as the paradise in which God had lovingly placed him.

Cherubs, mighty angelic celestials, were positioned at the east end of the garden to keep Adam from the tree of life and from the manifest presence of God. Cherubs are glorious creatures standing in the immediate area of the throne of God, adoring and praising the Eternal One.

After the fall, cherubs were ordered to stand guard at Eden's gate to prevent Adam from returning.

With the cherubs was a flaming sword that turned constantly. The sword was a separate entity from the cherubs, very much like a divine presence—moving, guarding, watching over the access to the tree of the knowledge of good and evil and the tree of life—the manifest presence of Life.

Adam and Eve were fugitives running from the manifest presence of God. The glory and beauty of the Lord's revealed essence became a fading memory. Man was shunned and rejected as a fugitive, an outlaw. He was a deserter, cursed to dwell far from his Designer, the one who gave him life.

Would Adam come to his senses and, if he wanted to, would he ever be able to return to God's presence? Would he, or his descendants, ever reconnect with God and have that intimate relationship Adam once experienced? What was the future to hold for mankind? Would man ever encounter the presence of God again?

CHAPTER ONE

STUDY GUIDE

SCRIPTURE

Read Genesis 3.

QUESTIONS

1. Adam and Eve were designed to live in a certain place. What was that spot?

2. What happened in that spot around dusk?

3. Why did Satan try to deceive Eve?

4. What appealed to Eve about what the serpent said?

5. Why did Adam and Eve hide from God?

6. What was the consequence of Adam and Eve's disobedience as it relates to God's presence?

7. Why were cherubs placed at the entrance to the garden?

REFLECTION

1. Do you ever hide from God after you sinned? If so, why?

2. Why does Satan try to deceive you?

3. Have you ever run from God or tried to hide from God's presence?

4. What is the Holy Spirit saying to you through this chapter?

PRAYER / CONFESSION

Heavenly Father,

I do not want to sin or hide from you when I do. I realize sin and failures when repeated often will separate me from your manifest presence. Forgive me of my sins and cleanse me with your precious blood.

I purpose to please you, obey you and walk close to you.

In Jesus Name,

Amen

MEDITATE / MEMORIZE

Now the Lord God had planted a garden in the east,
in Eden, and there He put the man He had formed.
Genesis 2:8 NTV

CHAPTER TWO
PLAN

A bel was tending his flocks and didn't see Cain watching him from behind the tree. Cain was very upset that God had not accepted his offering but had accepted Abel's. Hatred and jealously burned within him.

Cain had not given God the first fruits of his harvest, so his gift was rejected. Cain was jealous of Abel and saw him as the cause of his offer not being accepted.

God had visited the sons of Adam from time to time, and they had conversed with God similarily as Adam did. Cain and Abel regularly experienced some dimension of the manifest presence of God. They had developed a custom of approaching Him and communing with Him. On this occasion, they brought Him offerings.

The more Cain thought about how God didn't receive his offering, but did Abel's, the angrier he became. It was obvious to Cain that God favored Abel over him.

A RIVER OF BLOOD FLOWED FROM THE CUT CREATING A LARGE POOL AROUND HIS HEAD

Cain had convinced Abel to go with him to one of his fields. Cain saw his opportunity. Burning with rage, he grabbed a nearby stone and impulsively rushed Abel before he was able to turn, striking him on the right side of his head.

Abel moaned and fell to the ground unconscious. A river of blood flowed from the cut, creating a large pool around his head. Abel lost a lot of blood. And soon his organs failed, and he died.

The family was devastated. This is the second incident for the first family on earth where sin separated man from the manifest presence of God.

CURSED

In the course of time Cain brought some of the fruits
of the soil as an offering to the Lord. … The Lord
looked with favor on Abel and his offering, but on
Cain and his offering he did not look with favor.
Genesis 4:3-4 NIV

Instead of repenting for not bringing the first of his harvest, Cain had killed his brother in anger—bringing a unique curse upon his own life in the process.

God said, "You will be a restless wanderer on the
earth." Cain said to the Lord, "My punishment is
more than I can bear. Today you are driving me from
the land, and I will be hidden from your presence."
Genesis 4:12-14 NIV

Cain understood that he was being expelled from God's manifest presence. Cain was banished from God.

> Cain went out from the presence of the Lord,
> and settled in the land of Nod, east of Eden.
> Gen 4:16 NASV

What loneliness Cain must have felt! What deprivation! No wonder he said to God, "My punishment is more than I can bear."

Would this banishment be man's permanent legacy? Or would God find a way for man to return to His loving presence?

BANISHED

It displeased Adam's Father to see the human being He designed and loved so affectionately wander off into dark and dry places. He was unhappy that Adam and Eve disobeyed Him. Father God wanted the very best for them and to give them everything. Father's desire was to lavish them with His affection and attention. He especially wanted to have a very real, authentic, up close, and personal relationship with them. They were His precious children. He did not want to remove them from being near Him.

It broke Father's heart to see his son and daughter driven away into the blackness. God knew how hard the future would be for them and their offspring. Toil, labor, birthing pains, hardship, sickness, disease, demons, and death were all ahead for them. Life would be very challenging and difficult outside the safety, sanctuary, and secret place of God's revealed nearness. They were not created to live outside of God's manifest presence. They would not do well.

Now, their son Cain was expelled and banished from the presence of God. Twice sin separated man from God's revealed presence. Two is the Biblical number of witness. God was testifying to the consequences of disobeying Him—exile from His presence.

What would happen now? Man was not made to live outside the revealed presence of God. Would God restore Adam and Eve to their original place in His presence? Or would Adam, Cain, and the entire human race be fugitives from God's presence forever? If God was to bring Adam's descendants back into His presence, how would He do it? What was the plan?

Good news! Because God has a desire for intimate nearness with humanity, He had a plan.

> I will dwell in them and walk among them. I will
> be their God, and they shall be My people.
> 2 Corinthians 6:16 NKJV

HIS AFFECTIONS

Our heavenly Father longs to be close to His people. He wants to be near those He has chosen and those He loves. He wants to be near you. He loves and cares for you. God not only accepts you but also has strong feelings toward you. So strong are those feelings that He gave His Son to die in your place. It was that act that made it possible for you to encounter the proximity of His person and enjoy the immediacy of His companionship.

THEY WERE NOT CREATED TO LIVE OUTSIDE OF GOD'S MANIFEST PRESENCE

It is a sad thing that some Christians can live their entire lives and never experience this kind of intimacy with their heavenly Father. Your Father in heaven desires fellowship, intimacy, and a relationship with you. He wants you close to Him.

When John the Revelator saw the new heaven and the new earth appear, and the holy city, New Jerusalem, descending from heaven, he heard a loud voice saying:

> Behold the tabernacle of God is with men, and He will
> dwell with them, and they shall be His people, and
> God Himself will be with them and be their God.
> Revelation 21:3 NKJV

ORIGINAL PLAN

This has been God's plan—from the beginning God created man for fellowship. Even when Adam was driven from the presence of His Creator, God had a plan to restore man to Himself. He would make a way for man to be close to Him again.

Over the centuries, God worked patiently with the people of Israel to get them to be a nation of priests unto Him. He preserved and guided them through difficult situations so that He could have a unique nation of people who would commune with Him. He said to Moses:

> You have seen what I did to the Egyptians, and how I
> bore you on eagles' wings and brought you to Myself.
> Exodus 19:4 NKJV

God delivered the Hebrew children from Egypt so that they would worship Him. He longed for their fellowship. And today, God desires the same of you.

Since the day Adam was banished, God has had a plan to restore humanity back to Him. His plan is not just for people to casually make His acquaintance or to be introduced to Him with the hope of getting an invitation to heaven. He wants us to live in constant communion with Him. This is the message of the Gospel; this is the reason God sent His only Son into the world. He came to die for our sins so that we could be friends and fellowship with God once again.

This, then, is the plan of God's presence. He longs to be with His people, to father His family, to be with His children, to whom He can be close.

It is how God's story starts in Genesis, the "book of beginnings," and this is how it ends in Revelation, "the apocalypse." The story starts with Adam and ends with all those who will choose Christ as their savior in heaven enjoying Him forever. This is the theme of the Bible, the heart of the Lord, the plan of His presence. He wants a people with whom He can enjoy continual fellowship.

When we are finally at rest in the presence of our Creator and have the assurance that we never need to leave His loving arms, all tears will cease. In that day, there will be no more separation by death, no more sorrow, no more pain, and no more crying. What a wonderful way to spend eternity encountering and interacting with our Heavenly Father.

HE WOULD MAKE A WAY FOR MAN TO BE CLOSE TO HIM AGAIN

God has a plan, a provision, a proposal, and a promise for you. He has designed a way for you to know His intimate presence. He has made provision for you to have access to Him. He wants to propose something to you and seal it with a promise. However, first we must discover what God's presence is.

CHAPTER TWO

STUDY GUIDE

SCRIPTURE

Read Genesis 3

QUESTIONS

1. Why did Cain get expelled from the presence of God?

2. How many times has this happened before?

3. Was it God's intent for man to be banished from His manifest presence?

4. What kind of feelings does God have for us?

5. What did God want from man?

6. What was God's original plan for man?

7. How do you know God will make a way for man to be in His presence again?

REFLECTION

1. God has a plan for mankind to connect with Him. How does that make you feel?

2. Have you experienced sin separating you from intimate fellowship with God?

3. What is the Holy Spirit saying to you through this chapter?

PRAYER / PROCLAMATION

Heavenly Father,

I see your hand in the affairs of mankind and how you created each person, including me for your manifest presence. I don't want to live detached and distant from you. I am only happy when I am in your manifest presence.

Reveal your plan for me as I read these pages and discover more about your revealed nearness.

In Jesus Name,

Amen

MEDITATE / MEMORIZE

> I will dwell in them [insert your name] and walk
> among them. I will be their [insert your name] God,
> and they [insert your name] shall be My people.
> 2 Corinthians 6:16 NKJV

EVERYWHERE

God is everywhere here, close to everything,
next to everyone
- A. W. Tozer

3

BOUNDLESS

Father led the way up the hill to the place of worship. He turned occasionally to ensure his family was following. His sons followed closely behind him with the lamb in tow, and his wife and daughters were behind them. It was their regular duty to go up to the high place to offer their sacrifices.

It took quite an effort to get to the hill. It was out of town about a mile, and then it was a half hour walk uphill. It certainly wasn't convenient. However, every devout and determined worshiper spent the time and effort to go up the hill to worship because they were certain there they would be closer to God.

After killing the lamb and prepping it for sacrifice, father meticulously lit the fire and after a few minutes it was blazing. When he placed it on the fire, the smell and smoke rose into the sky. These worshipers hoped that God could smell their sacrifice.

They were hoping the hill gave them an advantage to get their sacrificial offering closer to God. They strongly believed God dwelt in the heavens, so the higher they could get to Him the better the chance of their sacrifice being noticed and received.

LIMITED

Throughout history, the gods of the nations were believed by some to have a particular dominion. They were present in one place. Certain territories or borders limited some of these gods.

The root meaning of our word "principality" is the area of government given to a prince. This is true in the natural and the spiritual world. Spiritual princes have governance over certain territories giving many cities and nations of the world their own unique personality. Each spiritual principality or power has a set boundary or limits to their spiritual government..

When I was in Haiti, I could hear worshippers beating their drums and calling on the voodoo spirits far into the night. The voodoo gods were real to those who worshiped them. Each god is believed to be unique, and some are territorial, limited to one particular area, practice or circumstance. Some ruled over the dead carrying them to the afterlife. Other governed over the ocean and its life. Still others ruled the winds and currents.

Some American Indian tribes hold certain places to be more sacred than others because they believe that one of their gods dwells in that particular spot. When an Indian would pass by a waterfall or pass over a lake he might pray to the demon or spirit of the lake and leave an offering.

Even the Jews thought that God dwelt in the heavens. They made their sacrifices on the highest available mountain, trusting that the smoke from the sacrifice would ascend to heaven. They thought that God could more easily hear their praises when they stood on a high place.

Some Christians have a very similar concept. They limit God to a building (a cathedral, for example) or to a particular liturgy. Most Christians feel closer to God in a building dedicated to worship. While it may be true that God manifests His presence more in places dedicated to worship, it is also true that He is everywhere. He is not more present in a church or on top of a mountain than He is in any other place. He is everywhere, always.

God is not more present in the church than He is in your home. Today, God does not dwell in temples made with hands but dwells in and among His people. Wherever His people can be found, He is there. Yet He is still everywhere, always.

God is present in the church. He is present in the grocery store. He is in your car. He is in your home. He is in the office. He is in the park. He is present everywhere. No boundaries can be ascribed to Him.

If His presence were to be limited to heaven, He could not fill heaven and earth. To say God is more present in heaven is to limit Him. As we are free to move about from room to room, God cannot move about from one dimension to another, for He fills them all. He is eternally limitless and boundless.

THEY THOUGHT THAT GOD COULD HEAR THEIR PRAISES MORE EASILY WHEN THEY STOOD ON A HIGH PLACE

IMMENSE

God's presence is so immense that no boundaries can be ascribed to it. He simply has no limits.

God is before and beyond all time, as He is above and beyond all places. Being from eternity, before any real time, He also must be without as well as within any real space.

If a moment cannot be imagined separate from eternity, then a space cannot be imagined where God is not present. God cannot be contained in the earth or in the heavens.

But will God indeed dwell on the earth? Behold, heaven
and the heaven of heavens cannot contain You.
1 Kings 8:27 NKJV

God is a place unto Himself. He that was before the world and before specific places is to Himself a world and a place.

God fills all spaces and places with His presence in heaven and in earth.

> Heaven is my throne, and the earth is my footstool.
> Isaiah 66:1 NKJV

If God has an infinite essence, then He has an infinite presence. An infinite essence cannot be contained in a finite place, for He is not limited by time or space. He is present absolutely everywhere and absolutely always.

LIMITLESS

He, Who is eternal in duration, is also boundless in His presence. The same thing that causes Him to be eternal causes Him to be limitless.

Not only is God's presence unlimited by place, He is also unlimited by time. Our heavenly Father inhabits eternity. He dwells in the infinite past, in the present, and also in the future. He has always been present—without bounds or restrictions of time. God cannot be measured or limited by time.

> For thus says the High and Lofty One Who
> inhabits eternity, whose name is holy.
> Isaiah 57:15

Because God is present everywhere, to maintain and to sustain, He can do it immediately. He is so present that He can work all things instantly. He knows all things immediately because He is present everywhere, so He can act instantly.

God does not require time to gather His tools. He is never delayed by the need to travel. It takes Him no time at all to identify the problem and to begin the process of repair. He is perfectly equipped, present everywhere, and all knowing. Nothing escapes His eye. He is perfectly present!

KNOWS ALL

God is immense. He is everywhere. He fills everything. He is in the deepest cells of every creature. He is present in every star of every galaxy in the universe. He is present in everything and in every place, both in the heavens and on earth, therefore God knows everything.

God knows everything because He is present with everything. He cannot be distant from anything, and nothing can be far from His sight. He sees everything and knows everything because He is everywhere.

HE KNOWS ALL THINGS IMMEDIATELY BECAUSE HE IS PRESENT EVERYWHERE, SO HE CAN ACT INSTANTLY

We humans know things in one of two ways. Either information is conveyed to us, or we must be present to acquire the information through our senses. God does not have these limitations. Because He is everywhere, both within and without all the extremities of the farthest and nearest reaches of heaven and the earth, and because He fills everything, He knows everything.

INDIVISIBILE

God's presence is unlike the presence of matter as we know it. If a vessel is filled with a liquid, one part of the liquid fills one part of the vessel, and another part of the liquid fills another part of the vessel. But it is not a "part" of God which fills one place and another "part" of God which fills another place. All of God is everywhere, in everything, always.

The Creator fills His creation. God fills the entirety of heaven and earth. There is no spot that does not contain Him. The whole of God completely fills heaven, and the whole of God completely fills the earth.

The essential presence of God is never divided. He fills heaven and earth. It is not part of Him that fills heaven and part of Him that fills earth. All of Him fills one place as well as the other. One part of His essence is not in one place while another part of His essence is in another place. He is undivided, and He is everywhere.

Although we divide eternity into past, present, and future, it is, in reality, one indivisible point. God is not divided. It is impossible for one part of His essence to be separated from another. Anything that has parts is finite. God is infinite, therefore there are no parts to His essence.

Parts signify composition. God has no parts. He is unique. He is all and in all. We can say that God is here. We can say that God is there. We cannot say that part of God is here or that part of God is there. All of God is here and all of God is there. He is altogether everywhere, not by fragments but in His entirety. This is the mystery of the immensity of our God.

The essential presence of God cannot be multiplied or added to, for that which is infinite cannot become larger. God cannot add to Himself, for He is as large as He can possibly be. He cannot be more powerful, for He is already all powerful. He cannot be present in more places, for He is already present everywhere. He cannot gain more knowledge and wisdom for He already has all knowledge and wisdom.

CHAPTER THREE
STUDY GUIDE

SCRIPTURE

Read Isaiah 57:14-21.

.

QUESTIONS

1. When the author said God is omnipresent what does that mean?

2. How do we know God is everywhere?

3. How would you describe the boundlessness of God?

4. What is the indivisibility of God's presence?

5. How is it that God knows everything?

6. Since God is eternal how would you describe Him in relation to time?

7. Because God is everywhere how does that relate to what He knows and can do?

REFLECTION

1. How does it impact you when you consider that God is endless, boundless, and limitless?

2. What will you do differently knowing that God is unlimited in his presence?

3. What is the Holy Spirit saying to you through this chapter?

PRAYER / PROCLAMATION

Heavenly Father,

You are undivided and unlimited. Your immensity makes me realize that You are all powerful and all knowing. With You nothing is impossible.

I praise You for your boundless, limitless and unending presence.

In Jesus Name,

Amen

MEDITATE / MEMORIZE

> But will God indeed dwell on the earth? Behold, heaven
> and the heaven of heavens cannot contain You.
> 1 Kings 8:27 NKJV

4

PRESENT

○─────────────────────────────────────○

Jason hadn't realized how far he was away from land. He had gotten lost in his thoughts as he headed east from West Palm Beach, Florida. It had been a long and hard week at work with the pressure of a company merger and the challenges that brought. He was so glad to be on the water, in his boat, away from work and its problems.

He turned the boat off, lowered the anchor, and after fixing bait to the hooks, dropped a couple fishing lines in the water. This is what he enjoyed the most—fishing in the ocean.

After a few minutes, Jason turned around to see the shore, but he couldn't find it. A little concerned, he looked for his compass and realized it was not in the boat. He then checked his radio and noticed it was missing. Someone must have stolen it when it was at the storage yard.

It was getting dark, and Jason's concerns heightened. The current was turning the boat, so he didn't know what direction he came from. Not being able to see any landmarks, Jason did not know where he was. At that moment, it started to rain.

Anxiety rushed in, conquering the feelings of happiness and contentment that he had earlier. It was a strange mix of emotions. On one hand, Jason was contented to be on the water and in the rain. On the other hand, he was alone without direction.

Water was everywhere. Though Jason liked water, right now it was over him, under him, to the left, and to the right. No matter where he turned there was water. It made him smile. However, the thought nagged at him, "How was he to get home?"

A few minutes later he discovered his new depth finder had a setting that gave him his location. With that he was able to head in the right direction. A few hours later, he arrived at the boat launch. After putting the boat on his trailer, he jumped into his truck and headed home.

PERVASIVE

Just as Jason was surrounded by water, so God surrounds each of us. Just as the water was all around Jason, so is the presence of God. He is not always seen or felt or heard or observed like water, but He is always there. Our God is omnipresent—present everywhere at once.

No place can be deprived of His presence. Since He fills everything, no place can be without Him. God is in every city, in every state, in every street, in every house, in every field, in every forest, and on every mountain. He is so immense that He fills everything.

MASSIVE

God is as massive as He is eternal. His indivisible existence reaches through all time and through all places.

As all times are a moment to His eternity, so all places are a pinpoint to His massive essence. As God is larger than all time, so He is vaster than all places.

Behold, the nations are as a drop in a bucket and
are counted as the small dust on the scale. Look,
He lifts up the isles as a very little thing.
Isaiah 40:15 NKJV

This immensity is not easily understood. If a man were set in the highest heavens, he would not be nearer to God than if he were in the center of the earth. You cannot be nearer to God or further from God, no matter where you are, for He is everywhere.

David was aware of the fact that he could never escape the immensity of God's presence. He said:

Where can I go from Your Spirit? Or where can I
flee from Your presence? If I ascend into heaven, You
are there; If I make my bed in hell, behold, You are
there. If I take the wings of the morning and dwell in
the uttermost parts of the sea, even there Your hand
shall lead me and Your right hand shall hold me.
Psalms 139:7-10 NKJV

Where indeed? God is always everywhere. He is not just "in" heaven or "in" the earth. He fills heaven and earth. He fills and totally encompasses, both outwardly and inwardly, the earth and the expanse of all the heavens.

He is present by His glory in heaven, comforting the saints who have gone before us, and He is present by His wrath in hell, meting out punishment to the damned. In heaven, He is spreading His love as a blanket. In hell, He is administering justice as only He can.

He is in all places, present with all creatures seen and unseen, terrestrial and celestial. He can be your constant companion and, at the same time, be the constant companion of everyone else who loves Him.

UBIQUITOUS

You cannot leave God's omnipresence nor return to His omnipresence. He is always everywhere, like the air around us. But He is so much greater than the air around us, for He is also present in the farthest extremities of space and beyond.

Since God is in heaven, He is with all the angels, all the cherubs, and all the seraphim. He is also present with all the spirits that roam the surface of the earth, hoping to influence (or enter and dwell in) beasts or men.

HE IS WITH THE DARKEST DEVILS JUST AS HE IS WITH THE BRIGHTEST ANGELS

He is present with the fallen angels and principalities that rule in the heavens over the cities and municipalities of the world. He is just as much present with the kingdom of darkness and all its principles as He is with all the redeemed who live in the Kingdom of Light. The immensity of God's presence is such that He is with the darkest devils just as He is with the brightest angels.

He is with the lowly dust, just as He is with the sparkling sun. He is equally present with the damned and the blessed. He is equally present with the good and the bad. He is so immense that nothing and noone are removed from or are outside of His presence.

We can never be nearer or further from God's presence. We can neither leave His presence nor enter into it. That particular dimension of God's presence is always (at all times) everywhere (in all places). He fills "heaven and earth"—equally.

As David discovered, if we could sprout wings and fly to the farthest reaches of the universe in a moment of time, we would find that God's presence was there before we arrived. What a thought! He is already everywhere, and He is always everywhere.

VAST

God is infinite in His being, so His presence is infinite. It has no beginning, and it has no end. He encompasses all and is encompassed by none.

The Creator contains the world, yet the world does not contain the Creator. If all things live and move in Him, then He is present with everything that has life and motion. Whatever lives and moves, lives and moves in Him. This is the "bigness" of the essence of our God.

The "bigness" of God is incomprehensible to the finite mind. The fact that He is so immense and that He fills everything makes it impossible for us to understand Him in His entirety. There is nothing with which to compare Him and no words to adequately describe Him.

If we cannot conceive of the vastness and glory of the heavens, how much less can we conceive of the greatness of God? He fills all the vastness of the universe, yet it is too small to contain Him.

No creature can exclude His presence. The Apostle Paul stated it aptly in his discourse on Mars Hill:

> For in Him we live and move and have our being.
> Acts 17:28 KJV

He is not absent from anyone or anything. He is so present that He is more important to life than the air we breathe. We do not live and move "by Him;" we live and move "in Him."

CHAPTER FOUR
STUDY GUIDE

SCRIPTURE

Read Psalms 139.

QUESTIONS

1. How would you describe the vastness of God?

2. How is God with both the damned and the blessed simultaneously?

3. What does it mean that God's indivisible existence reaches through all time and through all places?

4. Why is it not possible to leave or return to God's presence?

5. What is the objectivity of God's presence?

6. How is God's omnipresence comforting to us?

7. What does it mean that God is not only near all things but also in all things?

REFLECTION

1. How does it impact you to realize you cannot be nearer to God or farther from God, no matter where you go?

2. What does it mean to you that God's vastness is so great that we cannot comprehend it?

3. What is the Holy Spirit saying to you about this chapter?

PRAYER / CONFESSION

Heavenly Father,

I acknowlege your vastness and greatness. That you are present everywhere. It is difficult to comprehend how present you are.

It is comforting to know you are near all places and all things. I know you are near me. Thank you for your abiding nearness.

In Jesus Name,

Amen

MEDITATE / MEMORIZE

Where can I go from Your Spirit? Or where can I flee from Your presence? If I ascend into heaven, You are there; If I make my bed in hell, behold, You are there. If I take the wings of the morning and dwell in the uttermost parts of the sea, even there Your hand shall lead me and Your right hand shall hold me.
Psalms 139:7-10 NKJV

5

UNCHANGING

○——————————————————————————————○

It was about 450 BC, and Israel was continuing in their immorality and careless behavior, ignoring the warnings of the judgment God spoke through the prophets Amos, Micah, Hosea, and Joel.

Then one day, Malachi, whose name means "my messenger," came under divine inspiration and declared God's thoughts—warning the priests of their arrogance and contempt for God's Law. Then, God addressed, in no uncertain terms, the treachery of the priests and laymen in divorcing their faithful wives and marrying heathen women who worship idols and the demons behind them.

It is in this context that God declares, through Malachi, His unchanging nature. He wanted them to know that His love for His people and His mercy last forever. If they would repent and turn from their ways, they would not experience His displeasure. To make the point, God says,

> For I am the Lord, I do not change!
> Malachi 3:6 NKJV

This tells us that God's nature does not vary, alter, or amend. So His presence, as well as His power, is consistent and constant. God is immutable. He is unchangeable and unchanging.

> The heavens are the work of Your hands. They will
> perish, but You will endure. Yes, all of them will
> grow old like a garment. Like a cloak, You will
> change them, and they will be changed. But You
> are the same, and Your years will have no end.
> Psalms 102:25-27 NKJV

God is Spirit (John 4:24) and is, in all time whether past, present, or future and in all places, the same forever. So His presence is eternal and always constant, unwavering, and totally stable.

Change is not always good and not always bad. Some changes are for the better, while others are for the worse. But God can neither be any better, nor any worse. There is nothing about Him to change. He is perfect and maintains that perfect state constantly.

> Every good and every perfect gift is from above and
> comes down from the Father of lights, with whom
> there is no variation or shadow of turning.
> James 1:17 NKJV

Because God is always the same, His omnipresence (His all-presence) is the same. It is never altered. The omnipresence of God is the same today as it was at the time when Paul wrote his letter to the Romans, or the time when Moses led the children of Israel through the wilderness. It is even the same as it was during the time of the creation.

God's presence is perfect and, therefore, constant, never diminishing or dissipating. It needs no maintenance. He has always been solidly present, and He always will be. Nothing can change that fact.

POTENCY

The presence of God is a powerful force. Because He is everywhere, with everything He created, He is concerned for all His creation—never negligent, constantly vigilant.

God is aware of every need because He is watchful and near and, therefore, efficient in His caring. He is not everywhere just to be everywhere. He is everywhere to act. Wherever His presence is, power and virtue are dispensed. The Creator's presence is all-powerful, and that omnipotence is not without effective application.

God governs because He is present with all things. He governs by His presence what He made by His power. His presence and His power are together to preserve the created, as His presence and power were together when He first created everything. Every creature has the mark of the Creator upon it, and His presence is necessary to keep that impression valid.

Because His presence is unlimited, His power is unlimited. As His presence cannot be confined, His power cannot be confined. He is all-powerful.

Fifty six times the Bible uses the word "almighty." Almighty, however, is only used in reference to God. He is the Almighty. There is nothing that He cannot do. There is no limit to the energy of His presence. It takes God no more energy to create a universe than it does to make a flower grow. He can do one thing as easily and effortlessly as He can do another. He does everything effectively, without dissipating His strength. He never tires.

> The Everlasting God, the Lord, the Creator of the
> ends of the earth neither faints nor is weary.
> Isaiah 40:28 NKJV

God's presence never needs to be replenished, for it never runs out. He never gets tired, and He never faints.

There are two areas in which the power of His presence can be seen most clearly. One is in His ability to create something out of nothing. The marvel of creation is, therefore, the most potent evidence of the power of His presence.

> By the word of the Lord the heavens were made and all
> the hosts of them by the breath of His mouth. For He
> spoke, and it was done. He commanded, and it stood fast.
> Psalms 33:6,9 NKJV

Perhaps we cannot witness the creation. But the ability of God to redeem the lost speaks just as forcefully of His "almightiness" as does the creation. And we can all witness this marvel.

The second demonstration of God's power and presence is His ability to draw all men to Himself. His power in redemption might be more awesome than it was in creation. In creation there was no opposition, no devil to subdue, no death to be conquered, no sin to be pardoned, no hell to be shut, and no cross to be suffered.

The mystery of the Gospel is the good news that all this has been successfully dealt with—because God is and because His presence is potent. Nothing is too hard for Him.

Where God works by His power, He is present. His power and His presence cannot be separated. His power cannot be anywhere that His presence is not. For the power of God to act, He must be present.

His presence is not less than His power, and His power is not less than His presence. Wherever He exerts His power, there He is. Wherever He displays His might, He is present. If He were not present, His power could not be there either. And where He is, His power is evident.

Before the world was made, He had power to make it and to hang it in space. He was there; He was present. Therefore, His power acted.

Power is synonymous with the presence of God. The Bible speaks of "the Son of Man sitting on the right hand of Power" (Mark 14:62), that is, at the right hand of God. God's presence and power are so inseparable that they are interchangeable. His presence brings the demonstration of His power.

PURITY

God's immense and potent presence is pure, unmixed with anything else. Although He fills heaven and earth, He is not mixed with heaven and earth. Although He is present

WE CAN NEITHER LEAVE HIS PRESENCE NOR ENTER INTO IT

with all creation, His presence is not mixed with creation. It remains pure and whole.

A sponge at the bottom of the ocean is encompassed by the sea, and filled by the seawater. The sponge, however, still retains its own nature. God's essence does not mix with anything. It is pure.

The light of the sun is present with the air but does not mix with it. The light remains light, and the air remains air. As our planet turns on its axis, the light of the sun is diffused through all the earth. That sunlight pierces transparent objects, yet it does not mix with them. The light remains light, and the transparent object remains essentially intact.

Although God is present in all things, He is not formally one with those things, in the sense that he never loses His essence in them. He remains God, and they remain things.

God is not everywhere through conjunction, composition, or mixture with anything, either on earth or in heaven. His essence touches everything, yet it is combined with nothing. The finite and the infinite cannot be joined. Nothing becomes God simply because it moves in Him. Fish move about in the sea, but a fish is not the sea. A fish is a fish, and the sea is the sea.

Just because God is in everything does not mean everything is to be worshiped—as some have taught. Only God is to be worshiped. Everything else derives its life from Him. Although He is in everything, and everything is in Him, He is still God. He is not mixed with that which He indwells.

Someone who worships the created is not worshiping the Creator. The substance of the created and the substance of the Creator are separate. Because Christ is in me does not mean that I should be worshiped. I am not Christ, and Christ is not me—although He abides in me, and I abide in Him.

In the same way, although God is with everything and in everything, He is not defiled by anything. Because His essence is not mixed with anything, it cannot be defiled. Being with the vilest creature cannot defile the presence of God.

He created everything. Could He be more defiled by being with something than by creating it in the first place? Does seeing something imperfect, deteriorated, or rotten defile God's eyes? What could be viler than the grave or hell? Yet He is there—as we have seen.

According to the book of Job, Satan appeared before God and spoke with Him (Job 1:7). Could God have been defiled or could He have contracted some impurity through association with that filthy spirit? No, God's purity stands in the midst of filthiness. He is heaven to Himself in the midst of hell. God can be present with devils or with wicked men and can witness the grossest sins imaginable and still not be affected by what He sees.

An angel appeared to Daniel in the lion's den. Yet the angel was not stained by the experience of imprisonment, defiled by the stench of the animal pit, or torn apart by the sharp teeth and claws of the beasts. In the same way, God is not affected by the evil and rottenness He witnesses. He cannot be defiled. His presence is pure.

It is hard for us to imagine that God is present with us when we commit some secret sin. Yet He is, and He is not defiled by that sin.

The knowledge of God's presence should cause us to stop sinning. He is present everywhere. He sees everything that we do. He overhears everything that we say. He is conscious of all the affairs of men. Nothing is done in secret.

Most of us, however, instead of acknowledging God's presence and refraining from sin, try to deny to ourselves and others that He is actually there and that He actually witnesses all our deeds. How small our impression of the God of the universe must be, to think that He does not see and know.

He sees all. He knows all. Yet He is defiled by nothing. His presence is pure.

He is so present that He is more important to life than the air we breathe. We do not live and move "by Him;" we live and move "in Him." (Acts 17:28)

EFFECTIVE

God is present everywhere by His authority; all things are subject to Him. He is present everywhere by His power sustaining all things; all things are naked before Him.

He created all things in the world, so He preserves everything as well. Preservation is not completely distinct from creation, and God was present when He created everything. Therefore, it is understandable that He should be present with everything while He preserves it. David said:

> You preserve man and beast.
> Psalms 36:6 NKJV

The writer of Hebrews declares that God upholds all things "by the word of His power" (Hebrews 13). His virtue sustains every living creature to prevent it from falling back into that nothingness from which it originally came. It was first elevated by the power of God and must now be maintained by that same power. He is present with everything to maintain it, to guard it, to watch over it, and to guide its progress.

What wonderful peace and security that gives the created—to know He is close to us in order to keep us. Nothing can deter His preserving presence.

Our God manages everything. He is the gardener who never leaves the garden for a moment. He is present with every plant and knows everything there is to know about each. Nothing escapes His watchful eye.

Since God can create all things, He can restore all things. And no damage is too difficult for Him to repair. He can restore our broken relationships. Nothing is impossible with God.

God preserves all. If something lives, it is because God gives it life. Nothing lives apart from Him. He is life. If something moves, it is because God gives it motion. Anything and everything that exists does so because God gives it existence. If God withdraws Himself, everything ceases to exist. Nothing can exist apart from him. His presence created everything, and His presence preserves everything.

God is the center of all molecular structure. All things are comprised of Him. He holds everything together and gives everything form and substance. As His essential presence was the foundation of the first existence of things by creation, so it is the foundation of the continued existence of everything created.

In the beginning, He measured the waters of the earth in the hollow of His hand, stretched the heavens out from the land, measured the dust of the earth in a thimble, and weighed the mountains and hills on a scale. God's power and majesty are set forth in the creation and preservation of all living things, for they are achieved only by His presence.

CHAPTER FIVE
STUDY GUIDE

SCRIPTURE

Read Psalms 33.

QUESTIONS

1. How is it possible that there is no variance or variability with God?

2. How would you describe the potency of God's presence?

3. How does the immutability of God affect His presence?

4. How would you describe the purity of God's presence?

5. How can God be in the presence of evil and not be affected by it?

6. What keeps each part of creation from falling back into nothingness, from which it came?

7. What is the effective aspect of God's presence?

REFLECTION

1. What does it mean to you that God maintains with His presence what He made with His power?

2. What does it mean to you that God's power is synonymous with His presence?

3. What is the Holy Spirit saying to you through this chapter?

PRAYER / CONFESSION

Heavenly Father,

You never change. You don't transform and morph into something else. You are always the same.

Because You are constant You are reliable and I can put my trust in You. Thank you for always being present and consistent in your nature.

In Jesus Name,

Amen

MEDITATE / MEMORIZE

> For I am the Lord, I do not change!
> Malachi 3:6 NKJV

MANIFEST

Worship is about encounter–
coming into God's presence
– Jack Hayford

6

REVEALED

David kissed his cheek and said, "God be with you, father." Then the ten-year-old ran out the tent door, skipping into the hillside. His small harp, hanging over his shoulder by a string, bounced as he pranced off to do his chores.

Young David enjoyed shepherding, even though it was a menial task which women, or the youngest man-child, often did. David saw purpose and pleasure in it.

Little did David know, as he skipped into the pasture to lead his flock, that from his loins would come the Great Shepherd who would lead His flock.

David cupped his hands around his mouth and sang into the air. Sheep came from random places and followed him up the rocky hillside. After a few minutes he found an area that was lush with green grass. David sat on a large rock and watched the sheep graze below him.

After a few minutes he untied his harp and plucked it with his fingers. The gut strings resonated giving David a pitch. He opened his mouth and soon a song was born. David was so good at creating praise melodies to Yahweh. The tunes came effortlessly as he turned his affections to his Heavenly Father.

This particular day there was an excitement in David's spirit. He sensed that something good was about to happen. His heart was happy and filled with song.

He always enjoyed the fresh mornings of a brand new day. That is when he enjoyed singing the most. This morning he sang, "Early in the morning will I seek you! I praise you! I sing to you my prayers."

It wasn't long into his spontaneous song of praise that David sensed a heavy weight over his body. His eyes grew wet with tears. It was a sobering and reverential feeling. His eyes filled with moisture and overflowed forming rivers down his rosy cheeks. David bowed his head— too overcome to continue singing. He dared not move. His fingers stopped gliding over the strings of his harp. He remained motionless looking down at the ground.

David thought to himself, "He is here!"

The rivers of tears dropped into the dust forming pools of liquid worship. Careful not to look up, David began to hum the melody on his harp and rocked back and forth, occasionally placing his forehead on the ground. He could sense the revealed manifestation of God all around him.

David had experienced this transcendent sensation many times before. It would happen when he played his harp and sang new songs from his heart. Today the sense of God's revealed nearness was very strong and unusually heavy. God was revealing Himself to David in a way that was tangible and knowable. David enjoyed these moments very much—the encounters with God's manifest presence.

EVIDENT

Ever since the creation of man, God has revealed Himself to mankind in unusual and diverse ways just as he did to David. God has a desire to show Himself to people. He is a relational being and wants to be near those He created. That is why He reveals Himself to us as a Father. It has always been His desire to be close to man and to have man close to Him. He wants us to know Him. His heart is to disclose Himself to those He loves.

This brings us to another dimension of God's presence—the "manifestation" of God's presence. Because God can be sensed, it is sometimes called His "felt" presence. Others call this presence His "revealed" presence. It is simply called His "manifest" presence.

GOD IS PRESENT EVERYWHERE HOWEVER HE IS NOT EVIDENT EVERYWHERE

God is present everywhere. However, He is not always evident everywhere. He occasionally chooses to reveal His presence. When He does choose to reveal Himself to us, He sometimes does it in unusual ways. He allows us to sense His presence. Usually we cannot see Him or hear Him or even feel Him, in the natural sense, yet we definitely know that He is present.

To those of us who know Him, knowing that we are in the presence of the Lord of our lives and the Lover of our souls creates a very deep excitement. Nothing could be more wonderful and satisfying.

CLOSE

The Hebrew word for "presence" used in Psalms 100:2 where it says, "Come before His presence with singing," means before, at, or to the face of, in the sense of being in full view of, under the eye of, or at the disposal of another. This does not refer to the omnipresence of God. This presence is a much closer and more intimate sense of being before or in front of God, having His full attention.

God is not calling us to just be where He is. He is calling us to come before His face, into His full view, under His loving gaze. He longs to look fully into our eyes. What He desires is not a passing glance or a fleeting sight, but an intense stare.

When someone is staring at you from across a crowded room, it is amazing how quickly you notice it. There is an uncanny awareness that someone's eyes are on you, although you sometimes cannot immediately locate who it is that is staring at you.

GOD INVITES YOU TO COME FACE TO FACE

The eyes of the Lord are upon us. He longs to catch our eye. He longs to draw our attention to Him and to draw us to Him—so near that we are not only in front of Him, where He can look fully into our eyes, but right up "in His face." To Him, looking from across the room is not enough. He wants to be right there next to you. This is what it means to be "in His manifest presence."

IN HIS FACE

There is a phrase that some people say when they don't want someone to "hassle" them or to get too close to them, when they want to be left alone. They say, "Get out of my face." God's heart is just the opposite.

God is saying to us, come into the proximately of my face. Draw near to me with singing" (Psalms 100:2). Enter My gates with thanksgiving and My courts with praise. (Psalms 100:4).

Father wants His children close to Him, not beside Him, not in back of Him, not simply in front of Him, but "in His face." Get in the face of God. You will have His full attention, and He will have yours.

To be invited to get in the face of the Lord shows favor, partiality, respect, and acceptance. When the Lord says, "Come before My presence," He is letting you know that He has accepted you. He is giving you an audience with the King of Heaven. He is not just allowing you to get near to Him; He is actually inviting you to approach Him. God invites you to come face to face.

> For God, who commanded the light to shine out of
> darkness, hath shined in our hearts, to give the light of the
> knowledge of the glory of God in the face of Jesus Christ.
> 2 Corinthians 4:6 KJV

The face of God radiates His glory. It glows with His grace. It communicates to you His undying and never-ending love. Nothing could be more wonderful than to be in the face of God or, as the scriptures call it, face to face.

> So Jacob called the name of the place Peniel: "For I
> have seen God face to face, and my life is preserved."
> Genesis 32:30 NKJV

> And the Lord spoke unto Moses face to
> face, as a man speaks to his friend.
> Exodus 33:11 KJV

"Face to face" is a term that speaks of intimacy with God. In modern terms, we might say that they were so close they were cheek to cheek. Many of Moses' companions feared this intimacy with God.

> The Lord talked with you face to face on the
> mountain from the midst of the fire...
> Deuteronomy 5:4 NKJV

Even today, many Christians are afraid to get too close to God. They are accustomed to living their lives without God's presence. They are afraid to draw near to Him, some for fear of the unknown and others for fear that they will become too spiritual for those around them and might loose their friends.

The Christian life, however, is a new lifestyle. It begins the day we were made a new creation in Christ, and it must not end until we are in the ultimate presence of God. God is calling us to be spiritual all the time, to live in His face, to walk in the Spirit every moment of every day.

> If we live in the Spirit, let us also walk in the Spirit.
> Galatians 5:25 NKJV

> This I say then: Walk in the Spirit, and you
> shall not fulfill the lust of the flesh.
> Galatians 5:16 KJV

We are called to be spiritual, to walk in the Spirit, to live "face to face" with God. This is normal Christian living. Sometimes we consider someone who has a lifestyle of seeking God to be unusual. This is sad. Living close to God should be the norm for daily Christian life, not the rare exception. Will you join me in desiring His presence and seeking His face?

CHAPTER SIX
STUDY GUIDE

SCRIPTURE

Read Exodus 33

QUESTIONS

1. What was happening to David in the opening story of this chapter?

2. How do you know God wants to be close to you?

3. What is "the manifest presence" of God?

4. What does the Hebrew word translated as "presence" mean?

5. What does it mean to you to be in God's face?

6. Though God is everywhere how is He not evident everywhere?

7. Why do you think some Christians do not want to be"face to face with God?

REFLECTION

1. In light of this chapter, how does Psalm 100:2 "come before His presence with singing," take on a new meaning for you?

2. What does being in God's revealed presence mean to you?

3. What is the Holy Spirit saying to you through this chapter?

PRAYER / CONFESSION

Heavenly Father,

Reveal your presence to me. I desire to experience You more frequently and intimately.

Show me how to come into your face. Give me the boldness to draw near to You and abide with You.

In Jesus Name,

Amen

MEDITATE / MEMORIZE

> And the Lord spoke unto Moses face to
> face, as a man speaks to his friend.
> Exodus 33:11 KJV

7

APPEARANCES

○———○

The dark chaos was soundless and motionless, disordered and disarranged—a primeval waste-place. Upon this ocean of nothing the presence of the Holy Spirit instantly appeared. He hovered over the primal liquids and the dark abyss.

Although He, as the omnipotent Creator, was in the liquid waters, under the waters, and beside the waters, the greatest concentration of His presence floated over the vacant void. The Spirit manifested Himself and moved over the waters more than He did in the waters, under the waters, or beside the waters.

Then the Designer Creator declared,

> "Let there be light," and there was light.
> Genesis 1:3 NIV

God revealed His presence and spoke to construct out of nothing that existed previously. God manifested His presence and began to design and create all stars, planets, and suns; rocks and minerals; all plant and sea life; and every animal and bird. Then, He manifested His presence again to create a unique creature, whom He called "man."

> The Lord God formed the man from the dust of the
> ground and breathed into his nostrils the breath
> of life, and the man became a living being.
> Genesis 2:7 NIV

God's manifested presence put life into Adam and made him a living being. That life came from the power of His revealed presence. An unusual amount of God's essence was revealed in a concentrated place to design and create man.

GOD GOES DOWN

There are many examples in scripture of God manifesting or revealing His presence in unusual ways. These appearances were very tangible and could be discerned by the natural senses.

Perhaps you remember this event…

> Then they said, "Come, let us build ourselves a city,
> with a tower that reaches to the heavens, so that we may
> make a name for ourselves and not be scattered over the
> face of the whole earth." But the Lord came down to
> see the city and the tower that the men were building.
> The Lord said, "…Come, let us go down and confuse
> their language so they will not understand each other."
> Genesis 11:4-7 NIV

In about 2500 B.C., in the area that later became known as Babylon, Noah's descendants decided to build a great city, which God called Babel. The work went so well that they became giddy with success and decided that they would build a tower so high it would reach to the heavens. God was not pleased with their arrogance and felt that He must intervene in their affairs. The effects of what He did that day are still felt around the world, for He came down to confuse their language and, thus, to cause them to scatter throughout the earth.

The term "came down" infers that an appearance of God happened. He was there all the time by His omnipresence, but He decided to manifest His presence. This is what Christian scholars call a theophany, an appearance by God. His appearance here was not a pleasant one. He "came down" to investigate the pride and the wicked intentions of the people of Babel and to execute judgment upon them.

The "us" of "let us go down," is the same term that was used for the Trinity in the creation account. There is no mistaking this divine intervention into the affairs of man.

> WITH AN OVERWHELMING SENSE OF GOD'S NEARNESS, HE HID HIS FACE AND BOWED HIS HEAD TOWARD THE BUSH

This was the beginning of not only the diversity of languages but also of the diversity of peoples. For the first time, mankind was divided into clans, nations, and even various ethnic groups—all a result of the power of God's manifest presence.

> The Lord confused the language of the
> whole world. From there the Lord scattered
> them over the face of the whole earth.
> Genesis 11:9 NIV

THE BUSH

After that, God appeared to Moses in a manifestation of His presence.

> The angel of the Lord appeared to him in a
> blazing fire from the midst of a bush; and he
> looked, and behold, the bush was burning
> with fire, yet the bush was not consumed.
> So Moses said, "I must turn aside now and see this
> marvelous sight, why the bush is not burned up."

> When the Lord saw that he turned aside to look,
> God called to him from the midst of the bush and
> said, "Moses, Moses!" And he said, "Here I am."
> Exodus 3:2-4 NASB

I consider the burning bush to be one of the most unusual expressions of God's manifest presence in Bible history. God showed Himself to Moses in a bush that burned with fire and yet the bush was not devoured. He very possibly looked out of the bush and spoke out of the bush, indicating God was in the burning shrub.

How interesting! The angel of the Lord, a revelation of God, was in the fire. God was so evident and knowable that Moses realized He was looking at God when he looked into the burning bush.

Then He said, "Do not come near here; remove your sandals from your feet, for the place on which you are standing is holy ground."

> He said also, "I am the God of your father, the God of
> Abraham, the God of Isaac, and the God of Jacob." Then
> Moses hid his face, for he was afraid to look at God.
> Exodus 3:6 KJV

Moses knew that he was in God's holy presence. With an overwhelming sense of God's nearness, he hid his face and bowed his head toward the bush, which burned with the fire of God's manifest presence. Sometimes you might feel the same way when you have an encounter with the King of all kings and Lord of all lords. You are afraid to look up because you sense His overwhelming nearness.

SIGNS

Moses had announced to Pharaoh,

> "This is what the Lord says: At midnight tonight
> I will pass through the heart of Egypt."
> Exodus 11:4 NLT

The presence of God manifested in plagues. In this case, Moses was blamed, but the plagues were the direct result of the manifest presence of God. God would judge Pharaoh Ramses for his stubbornness and his refusal to recognize and worship Him. The plagues demonstrated God's ability to deliver His people and they demonstrated that His presence was with them.

Rods become snakes, water become blood, frogs, gnats, and flies appeared, animals died, people got boils, hail and locusts destroyed vegetation, and darkness covered the land (Exodus 7-9).

THE MANIFEST PRESENCE OF GOD WAS SO POWERFUL THAT MEN AND ANIMALS DIED

Pharaoh's magicians responded with artificial manifestations of power, human trickery devised to counterfeit the true miracles of God, and with the manifestation of demonic power.

When Ramses refused to humble himself before his Creator, God manifested His presence in one last blow:

This is what the Lord says:

> "About midnight I will go throughout Egypt. Every
> firstborn son in Egypt will die, from the firstborn
> son of Pharaoh, who sits on the throne, to the
> firstborn son of the slave girl, who is at her hand
> mill, and all the firstborn of the cattle as well."
> Exodus 11:4-5 NIV

"I will go throughout Egypt." Under other circumstances those words might bring joy. In this case, however, God's presence would bring death and agony of the soul to every unprotected home.

The manifest presence of the living God was so powerful that both men and animals died as He passed. The unrepentant Ramses and his subjects learned a hard lesson that night. The Hebrews, who had obediently applied the blood of a one-year-old, male lamb or goat to the side posts and lintels of the doors of their homes, were protected.

> On that same night I will pass through Egypt and strike
> down every firstborn—both men and animals—and I
> will bring judgment on all the gods of Egypt, I am the
> Lord. The blood will be a sign for you on the houses where
> you are; and when I see the blood, I will pass over you.
> Exodus 12:12-13 NIV

That evening, the powerful presence of God passed through the streets in Egypt, affecting each household: on those which were not covered by the blood, death and destruction, on those that were, the joy of life and liberty. Before long, the land was filled with screams and great wailing. The unbelieving were mourning their loss, and the believing were rejoicing over their deliverance.

> There was loud wailing in Egypt, for there
> was not a house without someone dead.
> Exodus 12:30 NIV

Having seen the manifestation of His power, Ramses let God's people go. God's revealed presence brought mighty Pharaoh to his knees.

CHAPTER SEVEN
STUDY GUIDE

SCRIPTURE

Read Exodus 11 and 12:1-30.

QUESTIONS

1. How did God manifest his presence at creation?

2. How did God reveal Himself at the tower of Babel?

3. What other appearances did God make in this chapter?

4. What is the Bible saying to us when it records that Moses, staring at the burning bush, hid his face because he was afraid to look at God?

5. How do we know that God moved with His manifest presence through the streets of Egypt?

6. How are signs and wonders evidence of God's manifest presence?

REFLECTION

1. What does it mean to you that God said He would go throughout all of Egypt?

2. What appearances of God's manifest presence in this chapter impact you the most?

3. What is the Holy Spirit saying to you through this chapter?

PRAYER / CONFESSION

Heavenly Father,

You have made Yourself knowable to man. You have revealed parts of Yourself to us and given us glimpses into who You are.

I long to know you as Moses did. I desire to draw close to You and know You better.

In Jesus Name,

Amen

MEDITATE / MEMORIZE

> When the Lord saw that he turned aside to look,
> God called to him from the midst of the bush and
> said, "Moses, Moses!" And he said, "Here I am."
> Exodus 3:2-4 NASB

8

MANIFESTATIONS

○──○

W e are free!" The women said excitedly among themselves as they walked briskly north to the Red Sea.

"But will Ramses' armies catch up to us?" You could hear the uncertainty and anxiety in their voices.

The slaves marched toward the border, determined to get out of Egypt, yet they knew their master's armies might be coming for them. The Egyptian Pharaoh was not going to let his slaves walk away free.

Moses didn't know that Pharaoh's army was in hot pursuit with over six hundred of his best chariots, and they were closing fast. Israel had reached the Red Sea, and now they realized their exit was stopped.

It was not over. God wanted to show Pharaoh that these were His people, and He was going to fight for them.

Pharaoh, in deliberate defiance to Moses' God, led the Egyptian army in his two-horse golden chariot. He was certain this was a sure victory.

"We will get these slaves rounded up and heading home, and then we can get the country back to normal." He thought to himself.

"Look there they are!" an Israelite yelled out, pointing to the dust that Pharaoh's war machines were kicking up.

A mother screamed, "We are going to die in this desert!" as she clutched her children.

The Israelites knew they were more than six times in number to the Egyptian army, but they were untrained and undisciplined in the art of war—especially hand to hand combat. The Egyptians were one of the mightiest armies of the world—highly skilled in the tactics of war. They had equipment for fighting—helmets, shields, breastplates, swords, and spears. Their chariots alone could mow down hundreds and hundreds of the Israelites with the power of their horses and their massive wheels. It would be an indiscriminate massacre.

In contrast the slaves were on foot and unarmed. A few farming tools and shepherd's hooks were not going to help much. Panic gripped the slave nation. Women and children looked for a place to hide.

It was at that moment that Moses lifted up his rod, and a great wind blew the Red Sea back to the right and to the left, forming two huge walls of water. To the Israelites' amazement, the ground between the walls of water was dry, so they ran forward into the watery cavern.

Someone shouted, "Look! God is fighting for us!"

The Angel of the Lord made Himself visible along with a huge vertical column of vapor.

The cloud was dark on the side of the Egyptians and light on the side facing the Israelites. It appeared as a huge fireball reaching into the sky, lighting up the way into the watery abyss. It seemed to always move as the slaves moved forward, protecting them from behind.

The mighty Angel moved forward and backward as needed to make way for and to defend the slaves. The slow and silent movement of the majestic column was an assurance to the slaves that God's presence was physically with them.

The mothers and children became calm. The light cloud was a barrier between them and their enemies. It was effective in concealing their movements. There was hope that they would survive this. God was not only fighting for them, but they could actually see Him. God had revealed Himself to them in a very real way, calming their anxiety, and had revealed that He was going to help them in their exodus.

THE ANGEL OF THE LORD WAS VISIBLE ALONG WITH A HUGE VERTICAL COLUMN OF VAPOR

CLOUD AND FIRE

As the children of Israel left Egypt and traveled toward the Promised Land, God's presence with them and visible. Everyone could see it. During the daytime, His presence was seen as a column of cloud and, at night, it appeared as a column of fire. None could doubt His presence! It was evident to all.

This cloud of God's presence protected the children of Israel.

> Then the angel of God, who had been traveling in
> front of Israel's army, withdrew and went behind
> them. The pillar of cloud also moved from in front
> and stood behind them, coming between the armies
> of Egypt and Israel. Throughout the night the cloud
> brought darkness to the one side and light to the other
> side; so neither went near the other all night long.
> Exodus 14:19-20 NIV

God Himself stood between the armies of Pharaoh and the escaping Israelites. The phrase "Angel of God" is believed by most Bible scholars to be an expression of God. It is not believed, however, to be Jehovah Himself but perhaps a manifestation of the Son of God, the pre-incarnate

Logos, in Old Testament times. He was with the Father in creation, and here, perhaps, we see Him again, long before He came to earth in the form of a man.

THE LORD LOOKED DOWN UPON THE ARMY OF EGYPTIANS

Whatever the case, it is a clear manifestation of the presence of the Lord. He was there to protect Israel.

> Now it came to pass in the morning watch, that the Lord looked down upon the army of Egyptians through the pillar of fire and the cloud, and troubled the army of Egyptians. And He took off their chariot wheels, so that they drove them with difficulty; And the Egyptians said, "Let's flee from the face of Israel, for the Lord fights for them against the Egyptians!"
> Exodus 14:24-25 NKJV

Even the pagan Egyptians had to acknowledge that what they were witnessing was the work of the presence of the God of Israel. Neither side doubted God's revealed presence.

PROTECTED

The presence of God in the cloud was a constant reminder that God was with them. When the cloud moved, the children of Israel were to pack up and move. When the cloud stayed, they were to halt their march and make camp. When the cloud descended, it was a signal to Moses that God wanted to meet with him in a special way.

> When the cloud was taken up from above the Tabernacle, the children of Israel went onward in all their journeys. But if the cloud was not taken up, then they did not journey till the day that it was taken up. For the cloud of the Lord was above the Tabernacle by day, and fire was over it by night, in the sight of all the house of Israel, throughout all their journeys.
> Exodus 40:36-38 NKJV

When we sense that God desires to call us aside, we should drop everything we are doing and rush to His presence. He has some wonderful things to say to us. Perhaps we don't see a visible cloud of His presence, but He will make known to us His desire to commune.

Aside from protection and guidance, the cloud served many other purposes. It protected Israel from the hot sun of the desert. Since it turned into a pillar of fire at night, the cloud became light for them in the midst of darkness.

What tremendous benefits we reap from the presence of God in our lives! He lights the way for us when we are in His presence. He will reveal things to you. His revealed presence protects you from the harm of spiritual attacks. Don't be without God's presence—even for a single moment.

Because Israel faithfully followed the presence of God in the cloud and in the fire, the Hebrew children eventually arrived safely at the crossing of the Jordan River.

SINAI

There are many manifestations of God to His chosen people recorded in the Bible. They show us how much God loved His people and wanted to be seen and sensed by them.

When Israel came to the desert of Sinai, Moses went up onto a mountain to meet with God. This mountain is referred to in the Bible as Mount Sinai.

> Then Moses went up to God, and the Lord
> called to him from the mountain...
> Exodus 19:3 NIV

As Moses went up the mountain, the presence of God became visible or manifest. He felt the nearness of God and heard the voice of his Lord.

On other days, the presence of God on the mountain manifested in strange ways that caused the people to tremble with fear. Thunder and lightning, the sound of a trumpet, and a thick cloud over the mountain were all evidence that God was near. When Moses led the people out of the camp toward the mountain to meet with God, smoke ascended from the mountain as from a great furnace. The sound of the trumpet grew louder, and the ground around the whole area shook.

THUNDER AND LIGHTNING, THE SOUND OF THE TRUMPET...WERE ALL EVIDENCE THAT GOD WAS NEAR

On the morning of the third day there was thunder and lightning, with a thick cloud over the mountain, and a very loud trumpet blast. Everyone in the camp trembled. Then Moses led the people out of the camp to meet with God, and they stood at the foot of the mountain. Mount Sinai was covered with smoke, because the Lord descended on it in fire. The smoke billowed up from it like smoke from a furnace, the whole mountain trembled violently. As the sound of the trumpet grew louder and louder, Moses spoke and the voice of God answered him.
Exodus 19:16-19 NIV

That demonstration of the power of God's presence was never forgotten in Israel. David remembered it as he sang before the Lord on Mount Zion many years later:

O God when You went out before Your people, when You marched through the wilderness, the earth shook. The heavens also dropped rain at the presence of God; Sinai itself was moved at the presence of God, the God of Israel.
Psalms 68:7-8 NKJV

Some people today would not have been comfortable at Mount Sinai. Some are uncomfortable when God reveals His presence by healing the sick and raising the dead. Yet these are all evidence of God's presence with His people.

Many people don't like loud demonstration. They are more comfortable when God is invisible and never reveals His potent presence. Surprisingly, some of Moses' companions felt the same way.

> When the people saw the thunder and lightning and
> heard the trumpet and saw the mountain in smoke,
> they trembled with fear. They stayed at a distance and
> said to Moses, "Speak to us yourself, and we will listen.
> But do not have God speak to us or we will die."
> Exodus 20:18-19 NIV

This was too much for some of the people. God was too present for their liking. Moses was a friend of God, but most of the Israelites did not share such a strong relationship with God. They were satisfied to hear from Him through Moses. This was too much for them.

What frightened some of them was that Moses and the elders of Israel were not only blessed by the presence of God on this mountain, they were permitted to actually see God.

> Moses and Aaron ... and the seventy elders of
> Israel went up and saw the God of Israel. Under
> his feet was something like a pavement made of
> sapphire, clear as the sky itself. But God did not
> raise his hand against these leaders of the Israelites.
> they saw God, and they ate and drank.
> Exodus 24:9-11 NIV

Many people have seen the manifest presence of God, but these men actually saw God. What an experience!

> When Moses went up on the mountain, the cloud covered
> it, and the glory of the Lord settled on Mount Sinai.
> For six days the cloud covered the mountain, and on the
> seventh day the Lord called to Moses from within the
> cloud. To the Israelites the glory of the Lord looked like
> a consuming fire on top of the mountain. Then Moses
> entered the cloud as he went on up the mountain.
> Exodus 24:15-18 NIV

Because most men were not comfortable with the manifestation of God's presence in their daily lives, God was forced to withdraw Himself to what they considered to be a safer distance. While Moses visited with God on Mount Sinai, God gave him detailed instructions for the design and construction of a place of worship. It was to be called a tabernacle or tent of meeting and would be a place where men could encounter the manifest presence of God.

Since the people of Israel, in general, wanted no part of God's manifest presence in their daily lives, He would contain it in a sanctuary and allow a privileged few, of His choice, to come before Him there.

TABERNACLE

The Tabernacle that God described to Moses was to be a place filled with God's holy presence. It had a specific purpose.

The elaborate preparations for the Tabernacle suggest to us that no detail of man's worship of God is too small for His concern. He is interested in men coming into His presence. This is, clearly, the most important thing in our lives.

Moses and Israel built the Tabernacle according to God's specific instructions (Exodus 40). When it was finished, the manifest presence of God came to dwell there.

> Then the cloud covered the Tent of Meeting, and the glory of the Lord filled the Tabernacle. Moses could not enter the Tent of Meeting because the cloud had settled upon it, and the glory of the Lord filled the Tabernacle.
> Exodus 40:34-35 NIV

Here, the presence of God was called the glory of the Lord. Later, we will discover the importance of the glory of the Lord and what it means to you.

CHAPTER EIGHT
STUDY GUIDE

SCRIPTURE

Read Exodus 14.

QUESTIONS

1. How did God reveal Himself to the Israelites in this chapter?

2. How did God's manifest presence help the Israelites?

3. What other ways does God reveal His presence?

4. How did God manifest Himself on Mount Sinai?

5. Why are some people uncomfortable with God manifesting His presence?

6. Why did God want Moses to build a tabernacle?

REFLECTION

1. What does God's manifest presence, revealed as a pillar of cloud and fire, mean to you?

2. Moses responded to God's invitation to enter His presence on Mount Sinai. How would you apply that to yourself?

3. What is the Holy Spirit saying to you through this chapter?

PRAYER / CONFESSION

Heavenly Father,

You are always near and everywhere. Yet there are times when You manifest your powerful presence to protect us.

Show us the power of your presence. Manifest yourself to us in our worship and our walk with You. Make your essence evident to those who desire to know You more, I pray.

In Jesus Name,

Amen

MEDITATE / MEMORIZE

> For the cloud of the Lord was above the Tabernacle
> by day, and fire was over it by night, in the sight of all
> the house of Israel, throughout all their journeys.
> Exodus 40:36-38 NKJV

9

CHAPTER NINE

ARK

It was a golden chest with celestial creatures on the top of its lid, and inside laid the Ten Commandments. The Ark of the Covenant was also known as "the Ark of the Testimony" and "the Ark of the Lord." What made the Ark special was that God revealed Himself in a cloud that floated between the cherubim. Therefore the Ark symbolized God's presence with His people.

The lid was called the "mercy seat" on which the high priest would sprinkle blood for the atonement of the people. But when Jesus came to earth to die for our sins He became the mercy seat and showed us mercy by being the once-and-for-all atonement for us. That day the Law was fulfilled. It is interesting that the Hebrew word for ark also means "coffin." It was a sarcophagus for the Law, buried once and for all and fulfilled in Jesus.

To the Israelites, the Ark was sacred and the center of attention in the camp. They considered it to be God's throne. It was at the Ark of the

Covenant that Moses and other ancients met God face to face. When Moses entered the Tent of Meeting to speak with the Lord, he heard God's voice speaking to him from between the two cherubim above the atonement cover—the Mercy Seat—on the Ark of the Testimony.

> So the people sent to Shiloh, that they might bring
> from there the Ark of the Covenant of the Lord
> of Hosts, who dwells between the cherubim.
> 1 Samuel 4:4 NKJV

WITHOUT THE ARK AND THE PRESENCE OF GOD THE TABERNACLE OF MOSES HAD NO PURPOSE

Because the Ark was so important, the Tabernacle was designed with the ark as its centerpiece. Everything else revolved around it. Three matching entrances led to it. Without the Ark and the presence of God that it represented, the Tabernacle of Moses had no purpose. Those who entered the Tabernacle did so because the presence of God dwelt in the Ark of the Covenant.

Once the Tabernacle was built, the Ark was secured behind the veil of the Holy of Holies, a room reserved for Moses (when the Lord called him to enter) and the high priest (on the day of atonement).

Throughout Israel's generations, going through the veil into the place where God dwelt was viewed as tantamount to suicide. Even the high priest entered the room with extreme caution. If, for some reason, he were unclean in God's sight when he entered the Holy of Holies, he would be immediately struck dead. Some scholars believe that the high priests tied a long rope onto one ankle and left one end of the rope outside the Most Holy Place so that the body of any priest slain by the presence of God could be recovered.

This has been a reminder to all generations that although God is willing to manifest His presence to His people, He does so on His own terms, not according to the whims of mortal man.

Traditionally, Israel sought guidance and direction from God at the Ark.

> Then all the children of Israel... came unto the house
> of God, and wept, and sat there before the Lord,
> and fasted that day until even... and enquired of the
> Lord, (for the ark of the covenant of God was there
> in those days).... And the Lord said, "Go up."
> Judges 20:26-28 KJV

God's manifest presence gives you direction for your life. He is your inspiration. Are you listening to what He is trying to say to you? Sometimes we need to be still and listen, even in prayer.

PRIZED

The Israelites never worshiped the Ark. However they treasured it as their most prized possession because of God's presence above it. The presence of the Ark was a reason for great rejoicing and, when it was missing, a cause for great concern. When it was returned after being captured the people rejoiced.

> And when the Ark of the Covenant of the Lord
> came into the camp, all Israel shouted with a
> great shout, so that the earth rang again.
> 1 Samuel 4:5 KJV

> So David, and the elders of Israel, and the captains over
> thousands, went to bring up the Ark of the Covenant
> of the Lord out of the house of Obed-edom with joy.
> 1 Chronicles 15:25 KJV

The manifestation of God's presence in the midst of those who love Him always brings joy. His presence brings us happiness and fulfillment. It is normal and Biblical to be jubilant when God reveals Himself to you.

> Thus all Israel brought up the Ark of the Covenant
> of the Lord with shouting, and with sound of the
> cornet, and with trumpets, and with cymbals,
> making a noise with psalteries and harps.
> 1 Chronicles 15:28 KJV

Dancing is another natural expression of joy in the presence of God. It is a joyful expression of happiness and praise to God.

When David danced before the Lord, his wife Michal was offended. As the daughter of Saul, she considered David's actions to be undignified for a king.

> And it came to pass, as the Ark of the Covenant of the Lord came to the city of David, that Michal the daughter of Saul looking out at a window saw King David dancing and playing: and she despised him in her heart.
> 1 Chronicles 15:29 KJV

David, however, could not let Michal's negative attitude dampen his fervor for God. He knew that God deserves the very best of our praise. He knew God delights in full-bodied praise. Her opposition to David's joyful praise and whole-hearted worship was punished with barrenness.

Praise was the natural response to the presence of God. Therefore, before the Ark of the Lord music was played constantly.

> …and Benaiah and Jahaziel the priests blew trumpets continually before the Ark of the Covenant of God.
> 1 Chronicles 16:6 NASB

> So he left there, before the Ark of the Covenant of the Lord, Asaph and his brethren to minister before the ark continually, as every day's work required: … And with them Heman and Jeduthun with trumpets and cymbals for those that should make a sound and with musical instruments of God.
> 1 Chronicles 16:37, 42 KJV

SECRET WEAPON

The Ark, God's manifest presence, was Israel's secret weapon in combat. The armies of Israel would take this box with them to war.

Joshua had the Ark carried into battle when he fought against Jericho. The children of Israel had no military power apart from the Lord. They had no trained armies and no experienced generals. For four hundred years they had served as slaves, making bricks. What did they know about armed conflict?

GOD'S MANIFEST PRESENCE WAS ISRAEL'S SECRET WEAPON IN COMBAT

Along the way from Egypt, they had picked up assorted weapons from the tribes they battled, but they could not wage war successfully against organized military powers—except that they had a secret weapon: the manifest presence of their God.

> Joshua got up early the next morning, and the priests
> took up the ark of the Lord. The seven priests carrying
> the seven trumpets went forward, marching before the
> Ark of the LORD and blowing the trumpets. The armed
> men went ahead of them, and the rear guard followed
> the ark of the Lord, while the trumpets kept sounding.
> Joshua 6:12-13 NIV

It wasn't long before the enemies of Israel learned the secret: with the Ark, Israel was invincible in battle. If the Ark could be captured, Israel could be defeated. The tactic of every enemy became, therefore, to isolate and capture the Ark.

> And when the Philistines heard the noise of the shout,
> they said, "What means the noise of this great shout
> in the camp of the Hebrews?" And they understood
> that the Ark of the Lord was come into the camp.
> 1 Samuel 4:6 KJV

When we celebrate the presence of the Lord in our midst, that lets every enemy know that God is with us and that we cannot be defeated. Every principality and power of spiritual wickedness in heavenly places is afraid of the mighty presence of God and is powerless to attack us when He is near. Every enemy bows in His presence.

When the Ashdodites arose early the next morning, behold, Dagon had fallen on his face to the ground before the Ark of the Lord. So they took Dagon and set him in his place again.

> But when they arose early the next morning, behold,
> Dagon had fallen on his face to the ground before
> the Ark of the Lord. And the head of Dagon and
> both the palms of his hands were cut off on the
> threshold; only the trunk of Dagon was left to him.
> 1 Samuel 5:3-4 NASB

At the presence of the Lord of Hosts other gods fall. The manifestation of God's presence has a chilling effect on God's enemies. Likewise the manifest presence of God in your life will fight dark powers for you. His presence will destroy evil plots and ploys targeted at you. What believer in Jesus would not want that kind of protection?

BEFORE GOD

When Solomon became king, he continued to honor the Ark and the God of the Ark.

> And Solomon...came to Jerusalem, and stood
> before the Ark of the Covenant of the Lord, and
> offered up burnt offerings, and offered peace
> offerings, and made a feast to all his servants.
> 1 Kings 3:15 KJV

Solomon knew that when he stood before the Ark, he was standing before God. He was in the revealed presence of the all-powerful Lord of Armies.

Since 586 B.C., when the armies of the famous Nebuchadnezzar sacked the city of Jerusalem and carried away or destroyed the Ark, Jews have felt their great loss. Some believe that Israel can never be great again until the Ark is found and restored to its place in everyday Jewish life. Much effort is given to its recovery.

As Christians, however, we know that when Jesus rose from the dead the veil of the Temple was torn in two by an invisible hand, signifying that all men could now enter into the Holy of Holies and encounter God's manifest presence for themselves, without fear.

Today, you are the Ark of the Covenant. God's glory rests upon you. You are the carrier of His presence. Wherever you go, the manifest presence of God can and should go too. God is calling you to be a testimony to the nations that God lives among those who love Him.

CHAPTER NINE

STUDY GUIDE

SCRIPTURE

Read 1 Chronicles 15 and 16.

QUESTIONS

1. Why was the Ark of the Covenant special to Israel?

2. How would you describe the Ark?

3. Who could carry the Ark of God?

4. What activities where done before the Ark?

5. What emotion is connected with the Ark?

6. How did the Ark of the Covenant impact the battles Israel fought?

7. How did Solomon honor the manifest presence of God?

REFLECTION

1. What does the Ark of the Covenant mean to you?

2. What would you do differently after seeing in this chapter how God's manifest presence impacted God's people?

3. What is the Holy Spirit saying to you through this chapter?

PRAYER / CONFESSION

Heavenly Father,

I want to know your abiding presence. I want to be a carrier of your manifest presence.

I acknowledge that your presence revealed in dark and challenging circumstances is a key victory in my life. I want to live in your presence and know You intimately.

In Jesus Name,

Amen

MEDITATE / MEMORIZE

> So he left there, before the Ark of the Covenant of
> the Lord, Asaph and his brethren to minister before
> the ark continually, as every day's work required:
> … And with them Heman and Jeduthun with
> trumpets and cymbals for those that should make
> a sound and with musical instruments of God.
> 1 Chronicles 16:37, 42 KJV

10

GLORY

○—————————————————————————○

We were about four songs into the worship service when I began to weep. This was a bit unusual for me to cry during a worship service, particularly at a conference where I was one of the guest speakers. I tried to control it, but I couldn't. The tears streamed down my cheeks.

I was at a Worship Congress in New Orleans. Mardi Gras was in full swing, and people had come from everywhere to celebrate. The streets were filled with drunken revelry.

Inside the conference, we also had reason to rejoice. About twelve hundred Christians attended that night. The church building was so crowded that some people were standing along the wall. The worship leader took us to a very special place in the presence of the Lord.

Everyone's faith was high as was the expectation of encountering God. We had sang, danced, and celebrated His goodness and Christ's sacrifice for us. But now there was a somberness in the room—a strong, lingering sense of God being near. The musicians continued to play very softly as people worshiped.

Before long, we all became aware that something very special was happening. There was a real awareness of God's presence among the people. We could sense God's glory and holiness. Some people began to weep, and some dropped to their knees before the Lord.

THERE WAS A SOMBRENESS IN THE ROOM--A STRONG, LINGERING SENSE OF GOD BEING NEAR

Long, tall men, most of them pastors, were stretched out across the floor in a row in front of the platform. Their faces were pressed down to the carpet, and their arms were stretched out above their heads, palms down.

Although there was no conductor, the musicians continued to play spontaneously. As the Lord gave each musician a melody, he played it. One instrument would crescendo for all to hear and then decrescendo, to blend with the rest, and another would rise.

I could feel the weight of God's glory on my body as we waited in His presence. I could no longer remain upright. I simply had to prostrate myself, as others had in front of me.

Suddenly a sensation of haughtiness and arrogance come over me, and I didn't like it whatsoever. So I quickly fell to my knees and continued to worship. But I still felt so lofty and proud. So I lay out on the floor in the aisle.

The sensation of my arrogance was strong. At that moment I felt a weight upon me—the weight of the glory of God. I dared not look up. The heaviness on my body was strong, as was the feeling of wanting to lower myself.

I decided to turn my head sideways so I could depress myself lower. My big nose was preventing me from humbling myself even more. Then I turned my feet outward so I can lay lower still.

There was a realization that someone very high and holy had entered the room. I wanted desperately to sink past the carpet into the cement foundation of the building. The glory of the Lord was in that place, and it had humbled me with the weighty substance of God's splendor.

Then, for a while, time seemed to stand still as we touched eternity together. Before the throne of the most awesome royalty we worshiped in the beauty of holiness, the only proper protocol. There was no doubt we were in the manifest presence of God.

At the time I could not explain what was happening to me. As I researched and studied the glory of God I recognized what I had encountered.

SPLENDOR

"The glory of the Lord" is a phrase very few people understand or can accurately define. Yet it is something we often read about in scripture and mention in our preaching of the Word of God. However, what is the glory of the Lord?

The glory of the Lord is a display of the excellence of God, the demonstration of His divine attributes and perfections. This is a reference to the manifestation of God's presence. Forty-five times the word "kabod" is translated as "glory." It signifies a visible manifestation of God. Often the word is associated with God's holiness.

God wants to reveal His glory, His splendor. He wants to disclose Himself to you. He wants to share with you His holiness—what distinguishes Him from everything.

GLORIOUS

When the Tabernacle Moses had built was finished and the priests were ready to begin their ministry there, Moses called everyone to gather before the tent for the dedication.

> And Moses said, "This is the thing which
> the Lord commanded you to do, and the
> glory of the Lord will appear to you."
> Leviticus 9:6 NKJV

They were expecting to see some physical evidence that God was present. Once the prescribed offerings had been placed on the altar— the calf, the goat, the grain, the bull, and the ram—something unusual happened:

> Moses and Aaron went into the tent of meeting, and when they came out they blessed the people, and the glory of the Lord appeared to all the people. And fire came out from before the Lord and consumed the burnt offering and the pieces of fat on the altar, and when all the people saw it, they shouted and fell on their faces.
> Leviticus 9:23-24 ESV

THE GLORY OF THE LORD APPEARED ... AND FIRE CAME OUT FROM BEFORE THE LORD

First, everyone saw the glory of the Lord, and then fire supernaturally lapped up the animal sacrifices. When the worshippers saw the fire and the glory, they cried out and bowed to the ground.

The glory of the Lord is a visible manifestation of God. It is something that can be seen. It is an exhibition or presentation of the splendor of the Lord, often seen as light. Light is a part of the nature of God, and when we enter His presence, the light of His nearness may fill the place where we are gathered. Others may see it in a different way—as fire perhaps.

Everyone that gathered could see this unusual manifestation of God's presence (Numbers 16:19).

> And it came to pass, when the congregation was gathered against Moses and against Aaron, that they looked toward the tabernacle of the congregation: and, behold, the cloud covered it, and the glory of the Lord appeared.
> Numbers 16:42 KJV

ALL WILL SEE

Someday, the Bible declares, the whole world will be filled with this manifestation of God's presence, His glory:

> But as truly as I live, all the earth shall be
> filled with the glory of the Lord.
> Numbers 14:21 KJV

The whole earth will be literally filled with the reality of His presence. His desire has always been that all men of all nations would recognize Him and worship Him for who He is. I believe this promise literally and hold to it in great expectation.

> The glory of the Lord shall be revealed, and all flesh shall
> see it together: For the mouth of the Lord hath spoken it.
> Isaiah 40:5 KJV

What an outstanding prophecy! All humans and all creatures will see the manifest presence of God. They will supernaturally encounter God when all creatures see His glory at the same time.

There will come a time when all living persons will know about the glory of the Lord. Everyone will be aware of God's manifest presence in the world. His presence will inundate every continent, every country on every continent, every city in every country on every continent, and every community within every city in every country on every continent. If people have not experienced the presence of God for themselves, they will certainly hear about it from others.

> For the earth will be filled with the knowledge of
> the glory of the Lord, as the waters cover the sea.
> Habakkuk 2:14 NIV

FAINTING

In several recorded instances in scripture, the glory of the Lord was so powerfully evident that some people could not stand up. They fell down in the awesome presence of God.

> And it came to pass, when the priests came out of
> the holy place, that the cloud filled the house of
> the Lord, so that the priests could not continue
> ministering because of the cloud; for the glory
> of the Lord filled the house of the Lord.
> 1 Kings 8:10-11 NKJV

Suddenly falling down while worshipping or being prayed for is often evidence of the power of the presence of God.

Some call this being "slain in the Spirit." The inference is that the Spirit of God has knocked them down. The presence of the Divine moving on the flesh of humans causes them to fall. Some people who fall in this way are unaware of what is happening around them for a period of time, sometimes for only a few minutes but sometimes for much longer. They lie that way for a time, while God talks to them and works on them; then they return to consciousness.

Many of those who have this experience later describe in detail something they saw or heard during the time they were unconscious. Some of them experience healing. Many of them have encountered the glory of the Lord. This can also happen in periods of deep worship.

> Indeed it came to pass, when the trumpeters and
> singers were as one, to make one sound to be heard in
> praising and thanking the Lord, and when they lifted
> up their voice with the trumpets and cymbals and
> instruments of music, and praised the Lord, saying:
> "For He is good, for His mercy endures forever,"
> that the house, the house of the Lord, was
> filled with a cloud, so that the priests could not
> continue ministering because of the cloud; for
> the glory of the Lord filled the house of God.
> 2 Chronicles 5:13-14 NKJV

The place where God manifested His glory came to be known as the "house of the Lord" or the "Lord's house." Everyone recognized His presence was there.

And the priests could not enter into the house of the Lord,
because the glory of the Lord had filled the Lord's house.
And when all the children of Israel saw how the fire came
down, and the glory of the Lord upon the house, they
bowed themselves with their faces to the ground upon
the pavement, and worshipped, and praised the Lord,
saying, "For he is good; for his mercy endures for ever."
2 Chronicles 7:2-3 KJV

The glory of the Lord was not reserved for the priests. We can all
experience it. Isaiah prophesied,

Arise, shine, for your light has come, and the
glory of the Lord has risen upon you.
Isaiah 60:1 ESV

God wants to share His glory with you. He wants you to experience
the brightness of your rising. Then He wants His presence in you to be a
witness to those who do not know Him as their Lord and Savior.

EZEKIEL

Ezekiel also saw the glory of the Lord but in a profound and unusual way.

Then I arose, and went forth into the plain: and, behold,
the glory of the Lord stood there, as the glory which
I saw by the river of Chebar and I fell on my face.
Ezekiel 3:23 KJV

Then the glory of the Lord went up from the cherub,
and stood over the threshold of the house; and
the house was filled with the cloud, and the court
was full of the brightness of the Lord's glory.
Ezekiel 10:4 KJV

Then brought me the way of the north gate before the
house: and I looked, and, behold, the glory of the Lord
filled the house of the Lord: and I fell upon my face.
Ezekiel 44:4 KJV

The glory of the Lord was seen also at the birth of Jesus. As the shepherds were watching their sheep that fateful night, they had a heavenly visitor. The Scriptures declare:

And, lo, the angel of the Lord came upon
them, and the glory of the Lord shone round
about them: and they were sore afraid.
Luke 2:9 KJV

A HEAVENLY ARMY OF LUMINARIES MARCHING AND PRAISING GOD WITH A SONG

Two things are notable in this passage, the angel of the Lord and the glory of the Lord. The two go together, as we shall see. In this case, the glory of God was so overwhelming that these brave men, accustomed to the night, being frequent companions of the stars, were now terrified by what they saw, and it soon got worse.

And suddenly there was with the angel a multitude of the
heavenly host praising God, and saying, "Glory to God in
the highest, and on earth peace, good will toward men."
Luke 2:13-14 KJV

First they saw the angel of the Lord and the glory of the Lord, and now they saw a multitude of heavenly militia coming out of the sky, singing a song.

Some scholars say that this was a celestial army of light-bearers marching from the sky lauding and boasting of God in a set discourse, a heavenly army of luminaries marching and praising God with a song they had previously prepared.

What a sight! No wonder the shepherds were awestruck, overwhelmed, and excited!

Several times, while I have been leading people in worship, I have had impressions of angels present in the room. When I opened my eyes, I couldn't see angels, but I was very aware that they were present, moving about above our heads and singing in loud voices.

This usually happened not when we were singing songs that we knew but when we were singing spontaneously in praise to God from our hearts. When we sing something that we know, we are thinking too much about the words and the music and not enough about Him. When we are not required to concentrate on a lyric and a melody, it is easier for us to enter another level of worship and see into another dimension.

According to the Bible, angels have musical ability and often sing adorations to the Lamb Who sits on the throne. The Bible also teaches that angels are very present with us. When we worship God, angels must get very excited, for angels are creatures of worship and of God's manifest presence.

The glory of the Lord was not just for the Old Testament. Paul spoke of it:

> But we all, with open face beholding as in a glass the
> glory of the Lord, are changed into the same image
> from glory to glory, even as by the Spirit of the Lord.
> 2 Corinthians 3:18 KJV

We can "all" behold the glory of the Lord. Although the great majority of Christians have not experienced it, that doesn't change the promise. We can all behold His glory "with open face," or with unrestricted vision.

Will you receive this promise? As you behold His glory, you are changed. A metamorphosis takes place in which you become like what you are beholding. We become like the glory of the Lord.

The more time you spend in the presence of God, the more you become like Him. You are changed into the same image. You progress "from glory to glory." This miraculous metamorphosis can take place in the Spirit and in the presence of the Creator. I encourage you to seek God's manifest presence, and perhaps He will reveal to you His glory.

CHAPTER TEN

STUDY GUIDE

SCRIPTURE

Read Ezekiel 3.

QUESTIONS

1. What is the definition of the phrase "the glory of the Lord"?

2. When Moses had finished building the Tabernacle, in what way did the glory of the Lord manifest?

3. How would you describe the glory of the Lord?

4. What are some instances when the glory of the Lord was evident?

5. What happened in those instances when God's glory was revealed?

6. How can we "all" behold the glory of God as the Bible declares?

REFLECTION

1. What does the glory of the Lord mean to you?

2. When have you experienced or seen the glory of the Lord?

3. What is the Holy Spirit saying to you through this chapter?

PRAYER / CONFESSION

Heavenly Father,

You are holy and exalted on high. Yet, You desire to reveal yourself to us.

I pray that the knowledge of your glory would cover the world so that every person would know your manifest presence. Show me your glory. Reveal to me your manifest presence.

In Jesus Name,

Amen

MEDITATE / MEMORIZE

The glory of the Lord shall be revealed, and all flesh shall see it together: For the mouth of the Lord hath spoken it.
Isaiah 40:5 KJV

11

THEOPHANY

───────────────────────────────

C ome father!" Gideon whispered softly. "Let's hide in here."

"Quickly!" He motioned to the cave. The Midianites had returned. They were a large tribe of fierce warriors, ravaging the country taking whatever they wanted. Gideon's family, and many other families, ran into the hills to hide from the thieving savages in dens and caves.

"Quiet!" Gideon, and his father and mother, ducked into the cave. After a few minutes he peeked out to see what the vicious robbers were doing.

Like a vast plague of locusts in broad daylight, the Midianites came as a gang of thieves confiscating Israel's animals, crops, and fruit, leaving behind very little to eat. The prowling marauders had destroyed the crops. Gideon and his family were devastated; they had nothing left and now were afraid for their lives.

The prophet had warned Israel this was a result of their evil behavior. God had had enough of their idol worship. He knew that honoring idols is honoring the demons behind them, and worshiping them would ultimately hurt Israel. But the pop culture didn't care and continued worshiping the "gods of the Amorites."

THE AMORITES WERE A VERY EVIL AND WICKED PEOPLE; MASTERS OF BLACK ARTS AND WITCHRAFT

The Amorites were descendants of the Rephaim (giants who were the offspring of fallen angels who had sex with human women). The Amorites were a very evil and wicked people; masters of black arts and witchcraft (the mysteries Satan's angels had shared with the Amorites) and had contaminated Israel.

The worship of the "gods of the Amorites" was the practice of the Midianites and now it was popular in Israel. God wanted to destroy the Midianites because of their worship of demon idols.

The Israelites were tired of their poverty and their fruitless labor. It was very discouraging growing crops only to see them stolen by their oppressors. Israel started to cry out to God.

The marauders had left, and Gideon and his father snuck out of the cave to see what was left of their crops.

"Here is some wheat!" Gideon announced.

"I will thresh it and make something to eat!"

"Then I will hide the rest so it doesn't get stolen."

Gideon placed the wheat stalks into the winepress and began beating it to separate the grain from the stalk. He didn't see the huge man sitting under the tree watching him. Gideon didn't know it was the angel of the Lord.

"The Lord is with you, mighty warrior!" The angel announced.

Gideon looked up in the direction of the voice and saw the angel.

"Sir, if the Lord is with us, why has all of this happened to us?" Gideon asked. It is what most people ask when they don't see God's perspective of their situation.

"Where are all His signs and wonders our ancestors told us about?"

"I think the Lord has abandoned us to let us fall into the hands of the Midianites."

The angel of the Lord turned to Gideon and said "Go in the strength you have and save Israel out of Midian's hand."

"But Lord," Gideon asked, "how can I save anyone? My tribe is the weakest, and I am the least of my family."

The angel of the Lord answered, "I will be with you, and you will strike down the Midianites."

The situation was serious enough that God had sent the angel of the Lord to change it. Things were about to better.

REVEALED

Gideon had encountered the manifest presence of the Lord because the "Angel of the Lord" was God Himself. The Lord appeared and spoke to Gideon, calling him a "mighty warrior." Gideon was shocked. He considered himself to be anything but a mighty warrior. The more they talked the more Gideon's attitude changed.

Gideon's confidence was rising, yet he wanted God to give him some sign to assure him that he was not imagining things, that he was really talking to God.

The Angel of the Lord touched the sacrifice that Gideon had prepared with the tip of the staff that was in his hand. Instantly fire flared up from the rock, consuming the offering and the angel disappeared into the smoke. At that moment Gideon knew that he had been in God's presence. He exclaimed:

"Ah Sovereign Lord! I have seen the
angel of the Lord face to face!"
But the Lord said to him, "Peace! Do not
be afraid. You are not going to die."
So Gideon built an altar to the Lord there
and called it The Lord is Peace.
Judges 6:22-24 NIV

Gideon soon defeated the enemies that had been plaguing them for so long and went on to become one of Israel's renowned judges or rulers. The manifest presence of God changed him from being the least in his own family to being the greatest and most respected man in all Israel.

The presence and glory of God can change the way you think about yourself, like it did Gideon. If you know that God is with you, you can face all sorts of obstacles.

HAGAR

The term "the Angel of the Lord" is a theophany—an appearance by God in human form. Most Bible scholars believe that the Angel of the Lord was none other than Jesus Christ, manifesting Himself in a tangible form.

The angel of the Lord found Hagar near a spring in
the desert. ... And he said, "Hagar, servant of Sarai,
where have you come from, and where are you going?"
"I'm running away from my mistress Sarai," she
answered. Then the angel of the Lord told her, "Go back
to your mistress and submit to her." The angel added,
"I will so increase your descendants that
they will be too numerous to count."
Genesis 16:7-10 NIV

The Angel of the Lord is an expression of the presence of God. It was God who saw Hagar in the desert and spoke with her there.

The angel of the Lord also said to her: "You are now
with child and you will have a son. You shall name him
Ishmael. He will live in hostility toward all his brothers."
Genesis 16:11-12 NIV

She gave this name to the Lord who spoke to
her: "You are the God who sees me," for she said,
"I have now seen the One who sees me."
Genesis 16:13 NIV

Hagar realized that the person speaking to her was not just a man. She called Him "Lord" and even "God." Hagar was not alone. She was in the presence of Jesus. He knew who she was, understood her dilemma, and resolved her problem.

THE ANGEL OF THE LORD IS A THEOPHANY--AN APPEARANCE OF GOD IN HUMAN FORM

ABRAHAM

The Angel of the Lord also appeared to Abraham on Mt. Moriah when he obeyed God by offering his son Isaac on an altar.

Then he reached out his hand and took the knife
to slay his son. But the angel of the Lord called
out to him from heaven, "Abraham! Abraham!"
"Here I am," he replied.
"Do not lay a hand on the boy," he said. "Do not do
anything to him. Now I know that you fear God, because
you have not withheld from me your son, your only son."
Genesis 22:10-12 NIV

We know that this angel is God because He said to Abraham, "You have not withheld from Me your son." Abraham knew that He was in the presence of God.

The angel of the Lord called to Abraham from
heaven a second time and said. "I swear by
myself, declares the Lord, that because you have

done this and have not withheld your son, your
only son, I will surely bless you and make your
descendants as numerous as the stars in the sky."
Genesis 22:15-17 NIV

AS THE FLAME BLAZED UP FROM THE ALTAR...THE ANGEL OF THE LORD ASCENDED IN THE FLAME

"I swear by Myself, declares the Lord."
If an angel had been speaking on the Lord's
behalf, he would have spoken in the third
person about God. He didn't. This angel was
God because He spoke in the first person.

MANOAH

Samson's mother also encountered the manifest presence of God. He
showed Himself to her as "the Angel of the Lord."

A certain man of Zorah, named Manoah … had a
wife who was sterile and remained childless. The angel
of the Lord appeared to her and said, "You are sterile
and childless, but you are going to conceive and have
a son." … Then the woman went to her husband and
told him, "A man of God came to me. He looked like
an angel of God, very awesome. I didn't ask him where
he came from, and he didn't tell me his name."
Judges 13:2-3 & 6 NIV

In describing what she had experienced to her husband, Samson's
mother called the angel "a man of God" who looked like an angel.

Later Manoah saw the Angel for himself.

The angel of the Lord came again to the
woman while she was out in the field.

…Then Manoah inquired of the angel of the
Lord, "What is your name, so that we may
honor you when your word comes true?"

He replied, "Why do you ask my name? It is beyond
understanding." Then Manoah took a young goat,
together with the grain offering, and sacrificed it on a
rock to the Lord. And the Lord did an amazing thing
while Manoah and his wife watched: As the flame blazed
up from the altar toward heaven, the angel of the Lord
ascended in the flame. Seeing this, Manoah and his wife
fell with their faces to the ground. When the angel of
the Lord did not show himself again to Manoah and his
wife, Manoah realized that it was the angel of the Lord.

"We are doomed to die!" he said to his
wife. "We have seen God!"
Judges 13:9, 17-22 NIV

At first, Manoah did not realize that he was talking to God. He asked
the Angel's name, perhaps thinking that it was a man. However, when the
angel ascended in the flame, all doubt was removed. Then, Manoah knew
that he had been talking to God Himself.

If people of the Old Testament could be in God's presence and not
realize it at first, how much more possible is it today for us to be unaware
of His presence with us?

Manoah had seen a theophany, a visible appearance or manifestation
of God. Perhaps it was even a "Christophany," the visible appearance of
Christ in a human form.

WARRIOR

There are several accounts in the Bible when the Angel of God revealed
Himself as a warrior. There is an account in the days of Hezekiah where
the Angel of the Lord appeared in order to annihilate an Assyrian army.

That night the angel of the Lord went out to the
Assyrian camp and killed 185,000 Assyrian soldiers.

When the surviving Assyrians woke up the next
morning, they found corpses everywhere.
2 Kings 19:35 NLT

AN ANGEL WAS SO POWERFUL THAT HE SLEW A HUNDRED AND EIGHTY-FIVE THOUSAND FIERCE FIGHTERS

The manifest presence of God, in the form of an angel, was so powerful that He slew a hundred and eighty-five thousand fierce fighters—a huge army of mortals.

David also knew that the presence of God could be powerful against his enemies. God's presence brings protection and puts the enemy to flight. David was aware of God's intervention in battle and prayed prophetically concerning his enemies:

Let the angel of the Lord chase them. Let
their way be dark and slippery: and let the
angel of the Lord persecute them.
Psalms 35:5-6 KJV

God's presence in your life will repel spiritual darkness that would try to come against you to destroy you.

Another account of God revealing Himself as a warrior was to Joshua.

When Joshua was near Jericho, he looked
up and saw a man standing in front of him
with a drawn sword in his hand.
Joshua 5:13 NIV

As happened other times, Joshua thought the Angel was a man. He looked so much like a man that Joshua approached him and asked, "Are you for us or for our enemies?"

"Neither," he replied, "But as commander of the army of the Lord I have now come." (Joshua 5:14 NIV)

Angels are warriors. But this was not simply an angelic warrior. This was the Commander Himself, He who orders the armies of heaven, He who gives commands to the luminaries. At this point, Joshua behaved differently.

> Then Joshua fell facedown to the ground in reverence,
> and asked him, "What message does my Lord have
> for his servant?" The commander of the Lord's army
> replied, "Take off your sandals, for the place where
> you are standing is holy." And Joshua did so.
> Joshua 5:14-15 NIV

Joshua witnessed a theophany, a representation of the presence of the Lord in a physical form.

Joshua's response to seeing God was the same as most others who witnessed such an awesome divine visitation. He fell face down to the ground in a posture of worship.

JESUS

When Jesus was resurrected from the dead, the Angel of the Lord was involved.

> There was a great earthquake: for the angel of the
> Lord descended from heaven, and came and rolled
> back the stone from the door, and sat upon it.
> Matthew 28:2 KJV

Could this be the presence of the divine at the tomb? Shafts of light were darting from his face and his clothes glistened brilliant white.

> His countenance was like lightning, and his
> raiment white as snow: and for fear of him the
> keepers did shake, and became as dead men.
> Matthew 28:3-4 KJV

The manifest presence of God greatly impacted these elite Roman soldiers! Overcome by terror, they fainted like feeble old ladies when suddenly confronted by God's presence as an angel.

PETER

The angel of the Lord also delivered Jesus' disciples from prison in Jerusalem.

> But during the night an angel of the Lord
> opened the doors of the jail and brought them
> out. "Go, stand in the temple courts," he said,
> "and tell the people all about this new life."
> Acts 5:19-20 NIV

Later, the angel of the Lord delivered Peter.

> The angel of the Lord came upon him, and a
> light shined in the prison: and he smote Peter
> on the side, and raised him up, saying, Arise up
> quickly. And his chains fell off from his hands.
> Acts 12:7 KJV

The angel of the Lord also spoke to Philip, the evangelist, giving him instructions on where he should go.

> And the angel of the Lord spoke to Philip,
> saying, "Arise, and go toward the south."
> Acts 8:26 KJV

In these New Testament cases, it is not as clear that the Scriptures refer to God. These men saw and spoke with a celestial creature from the presence of God. We cannot be certain that the angel of the Lord in the New Testament has the same weight as the angel of the Lord of the Old Testament, Who was clearly a manifestation of God's presence and, in most cases, the pre-incarnate Christ Himself.

It is clear that God wants to reveal Himself to mankind and chooses those times and places to fulfill His will. He also wants to reveal Himself to you to encourage you and to speak to you. So let God know you want to meet with Him and know Him better. He is your Angel.

CHAPTER ELEVEN
STUDY GUIDE

SCRIPTURE

Read Judges 6.

QUESTIONS

1. Who is "the angel of the Lord"?

2. What is a theophany?

3. How is the angel of the Lord related to God's manifest presence?

4. To whom did the angel of the Lord reveal Himself?

5. Joshua encountered a theophany. How would you describe it?

6. What are other names for this manifestation of God's presence known as "the angel of the Lord?"

7. What kind of encounter with God's manifest presence did Peter experience?

REFLECTION

1. What account of the appearance of the "angel of Lord" impacted you the most? Why?

2. How does it affect you to know Jesus visited men in history as an angel?

3. What is the Holy Spirit saying to you through this chapter?

PRAYER / CONFESSION

Heavenly Father,

You have revealed yourself in human form in the past. Reveal yourself to me in a way I can discern it is You.

You are my angel and I want to speak with You and know You better. This is my heart's cry.

In Jesus Name,

Amen

MEDITATE / MEMORIZE

> There was a great earthquake: for the angel of the
> Lord descended from heaven, and came and rolled
> back the stone from the door, and sat upon it.
> Matthew 28:2 KJV

12

LORD OF ARMIES

○──○

He could feel the ground shake through the straw mat he was sleeping on. Startled, Elisha's assistant jumped up and ran outside. He didn't see anything inside the city but he knew something powerful was taking place. There it was again. He ran to the top of the hill to see if he could see what was shaking the ground. He rubbed his eyes to focus, and when he opened them again he saw a massive army of footmen, horsemen, and chariots surrounding the city.

Elisha's personal assistant gasped and ran back to tell Elisha what he saw.

"What will we do?" The assistant asked. Elisha knew he was alarmed at seeing his town surrounded by hostile forces. They were there to capture Elisha. Paralyzed with debilitating fear, the assistant anticipated his death or the sudden capture of his mentor. He desperately wanted to know how they could save themselves.

Elisha's servant was new at working with Elisha and probably didn't know the supernatural powers God had given him. Even if he heard of Elisha's miracles, this enemy was present in overwhelming numbers and Elisha was only one man.

THESE ANGELIC WARRIORS HAD TAKEN ON THE FORM OF HORSE DRAWN CHARIOTS

Seeing his assistant's fear, Elisha quickly responded, "Oh, those with us are many more than those with our enemies."

"What do you mean?" The servant queried.

"Those that are with us to protect us are more than those that are against us to destroy us."

"Jehovah, open his eyes that he may see those that fight for us!" Elisha prayed wanting his assistant to see the army that fights for God's people.

His assistant thought, "That is a strange request!"

Suddenly his eyes, though already open, were able to see what he had never seen before. He gasped! What he saw on the range of hills behind the enemy army, and nearby around Elisha, were countless numbers of horses and chariots glowing and shining with the presence of God.

The assistant gasped and quickly raised his hands to his head and said, "Oh my!"

The heavenly army of angels burned with the power and presence of God. These angelic warriors had taken on the form of horse drawn chariots signifying their strength and supremacy.

They had come in response to Elisha's faith for he knew that angels were servants of God commissioned to assist Yahweh's followers. He knew that God was the commander of His mighty celestial armies because His name is The Lord of Hosts.

LORD OF ARMIES

The phrase "the Lord of Hosts" is a military term meaning "the Lord of armies" or "the captain of armies." The word "hosts" refers to a mass of persons, especially organized for war (an army), a campaign, company, or soldiers ready for war.

The name "Lord of Hosts" is a technical term signifying "Yahweh, the mightiest warrior," or "Yahweh, the all-powerful King." The name affirms God's universal kingship that encompasses every force or army, whether heavenly or earthly. The name points to Jehovah of Hosts, the Lord Almighty, and the King of Glory.

The concept that God is the commander of heavenly armies was not new to Hebrew thought. Israelites believed God was the sovereign commander of an innumerable mass of celestial beings organized and prepared for battle.

Jacob also encountered a huge group of angels and called them God's camp (Gen 32:1).

The Lord of Hosts is God's throne name, His royal name.

> ...I saw the sovereign master seated on a high, elevated
> throne. The hem of his robe filled the temple. Seraphs
> stood over him. ... They called out to one another,
> "Holy, holy, holy is the Lord who commands armies!
> His majestic splendor fills the entire earth!"
> Isaiah 6:1-3 NET

This name was associated with the Ark of the Covenant, where God was believed to maintain His throne. The name represents God's manifest presence.

> David arose, and went... to bring up... the ark
> of God, whose name is called by the name of the
> Lord of hosts that dwells between the cherubim.
> 2 Samuel 6:2 NKJV

SHILOH

Shiloh was special because God's presence was visibly evident there above the Ark of the Covenant, between the golden cherubim.

> This man went up out of his city yearly to worship
> and to sacrifice unto the Lord of hosts in Shiloh.
> 1 Samuel 1:3a NKJV

Those who went there went with an awareness they were approaching the Lord of Hosts—the all-powerful Lord of angelic armies.

This name, "Lord of Hosts," is also the name associated with God's glory. It is related to His Shekinah.

> So they sent men to Shiloh to bring the Ark of
> the Covenant of the Lord of Heaven's Armies,
> who is enthroned between the cherubim.
> 1 Samuel 4:4a NLT

When the people stood before the Ark, they could sense the power of the Lord of all Armies. The name connects the might of God's military with mankind.

DAVID

David used that name to defeat the giant Goliath.

> Then said David to the Philistine, "You come to me
> with a sword, with a spear, and with a javelin. But
> I come to you in the name of the Lord of hosts, the
> God of the armies of Israel, whom you have defied.
> 1 Samuel 17:45 NKJV

Goliath, though big in stature, was no match for the Lord of all Armies, the mightiest conqueror in heaven and earth. Goliath laughed, thinking that he was facing a mere boy, but he perished when he came face to face with the power of the presence of the Lord of Hosts.

Watch out, enemies of God! When the Lord of Hosts stirs His armies for battle, you have no chance.

> A sound of tumult on the mountains, Like
> that of many people! A sound of the uproar of

kingdoms, of nations gathered together! The Lord
of hosts is mustering the army for battle.
Isaiah 13:4 NASB

One day, the Mightiest of Warriors will shake the material universe to
its foundation. The captain of the Lord's armies will give the command,
and angelic fighters will go out to battle.

Therefore I will shake the heavens, and
the earth shall remove out of her place,
in the wrath of the Lord of hosts,
and in the day of His fierce anger.
Isaiah 13:13 NKJV

> **THE CAPTAIN OF THE LORD'S ARMIES WILL GIVE THE COMMAND AND ANGELIC FIGHTERS WILL GO OUT TO BATTLE**

There is also the ability to bless in the
powerful name "Lord of Hosts," as David did:

As soon as David had made an end of offering
burnt offerings and peace offerings, he blessed
the people in the name of the Lord of hosts.
2 Samuel 6:18 NKJV

The Bible declares there is fervor, enthusiasm, and intensity in this
name:

For out of Jerusalem shall go forth a remnant,
and they that escape out of mount Zion: the
zeal of the Lord of hosts shall do this.
2 Kings 19:31 NKJV

PROMISES

God has promised that the power and authority of our victorious
Champion is present to keep us safe. There is safety and protection in the
name "Lord of Hosts."

The Lord of hosts is with us; the God
of Jacob is our refuge. Selah
Psalms 46:7 NKJV

The promise of God's presence in the future, as the Lord of Hosts, can be found throughout Scripture. This name is repeated over and over, letting us know that He is the commander of all angel armies.

> Then… the Lord of hosts shall reign in mount Zion,
> and in Jerusalem, and before His ancients gloriously.
> Isaiah 24:23 NKJV

> Yea, many people and strong nations shall
> come to seek the Lord of hosts in Jerusalem,
> and to pray before the Lord.
> Zechariah 8:22 NKJV

What God is conveying to us in this name—the "Lord of Hosts"—is that He promises to be with us and protect us as the commander–in–chief of all of heaven's and earth's armies. When we encounter the God of angel armies, it is an encounter with God's revealed power and protection.

You are protected and guarded by the commander of angel armies. Angels are commissioned by the Holy Sovereign to protect and preserve His precious ones—His children, the innocent, the widow, the fatherless, and the orphan.

CHAPTER TWELVE
STUDY GUIDE

SCRIPTURE

Read 2 Kings 6.

QUESTIONS

1. What does the title "Lord of Hosts" mean?

2. What armies do you think God is in charge of?

3. What is the connection with the name "Lord of Hosts" and the Ark of the Covenant?

4. Why did David use the name "Lord of Armies" when fighting Goliath?

5. How is the name the "Lord of Hosts" connected to God's presence?

6. What promise or assurance can we receive from the name "Lord of Hosts?"

REFLECTION

1. What does the name the "Lord of Hosts" mean to you?

2. How will you think differently as a result of knowing God is a commander of angel armies?

3. What is the Holy Spirit saying to you through this chapter?

PRAYER / CONFESSION

Heavenly Father,

I acknowledge that You are the commander of angel armies. Though I cannot see them I am aware they are real and protect your people.

I am grateful that your armies are powerful and present protecting and serving me and my family. May they accomplish your justice and purpose in the earth.

In Jesus Name,

Amen

MEDITATE / MEMORIZE

> A sound of tumult on the mountains, Like
> that of many people! A sound of the uproar of
> kingdoms, of nations gathered together! The Lord
> of hosts is mustering the army for battle.
> Isaiah 13:4 NASB

13

PRESENCES

Jonah was resting on the top of his house when he heard Jehovah call his name. "Jonah!"

"Yes my Lord!" Jonah quickly stood up, facing the direction the voice was coming from.

"I want you to go to Nineveh and preach to its residents so they may repent. Their wickedness has come up before me" (Jonah 1:2).

Jonah froze for a moment then immediately turned away from the voice and darted out of his house, out of the city, and headed west to the seaport of Joppa.

Jonah didn't like what God had told him. He didn't want to see the evil people of Nineveh repent and receive God's forgiveness. They had corrupted and killed his people and wanted to conquer them. Jonah wanted to see revenge and vengeance taken out on them—not forgive them.

VOICE

So Jonah ran from the voice of the Lord—the manifest presence of God.

WHEN YOU FLEE GOD'S PRESENCE, YOU WILL ALWAYS GO DOWN-- BECOMING INSTANTLY VULNERABLE TO TRADGEDY

Jonah defied His voice and ran in the opposite direction from Nineveh. Jonah ran west, about fifty miles, till he reached the Mediterranean Sea. There he bought a ticket to Tarshish in Western Spain. That was the farthest point west in the known world. He just wanted to get as far away from his calling as he could.

Disobedient and defiant, Jonah ran from the face of God and went down to Joppa. When you flee the blessing and protection of God's presence, you will always go down—becoming instantly vulnerable to tragedy. What kind of life do we have when we flee "Life?" What good can we experience when we run from "Goodness?" How dim the light, when we shrink from the "Light of the World."

In God's love and mercy, He sends calamity to drive the fugitive back into His good and perfect will. God hurls stormy winds and threatening waves to rock not only Jonah's life but also the boat he was in. Jonah hides in the boat's belly and curls up in a fetal position, exhausted, and falls asleep.

Jonah was a worshiper and had known God's presence, but now he was not repentant, fleeing God's call on his life. Our disobedience will interrupt and disrupt our lives and the lives of those around us. The terrified crew chose to draw straws to see who was responsible for the storm. God further pressed Jonah and caused him to get the shorter straw. So they threw Jonah overboard because they knew he was running from God and was the source of their danger. When his body hit the water, the storm and sea immediately calmed.

Jonah's body sank quickly to the bottom. Seaweed wrapped around his head. Soon there was only a breath between him and death. Jonah was now a drowning man entangled in seaweed. The rebel fugitive had come to the end of his escape. There was nowhere else to go. He had reached the end of himself and was about to die.

Just then a four-thousand-pound white shark (as some historians believe, because there are no whales in the Mediterranean Sea) swallowed Jonah. Now Jonah was no longer in the belly of a boat but the belly of a fish. Things were getting worse for the runaway.

It was only in this extreme situation—after three days and three nights in darkness and dankness, mucus and membranes, tossing and turning in the shark's stomach—that the spirit of the rebel was broken.

Jonah, imprisoned in a shark's stomach, lifted up his voice and sang a prayer of thanksgiving to His God. He did not petition or beg God for life and deliverance. He simply thanked Him for Who He is and what He means to him. Out of the belly of death, Jonah sang blessings to God and God heard him. Jonah, just like Paul and Silas, was delivered from dire circumstances when he sang prayers.

The Book of Jonah is a picture of those who, when God calls, they disobey Him. It is an image of how He deals with us, yet does not abandon us. He lets us run to the end of ourselves and have our way for a time; then He surrounds us with difficulties so that we will eventually run back to a "God once displeased," a "God appeased."

The voice was a manifestation of God's revealed presence. Jonah simply ran from God's presence.

VOICES

Samuel had a similar experience, however he ran into the presence of the voice.

> The Lord called Samuel again the third
> time. Then he arose and went to Eli, and
> said, "Here I am, for you did call me."
> Then Eli perceived that the Lord had called the
> boy. Therefore Eli said to Samuel, "Go, lie down;

> and it shall be, if He calls you, that you must
> say, 'Speak, Lord, for your servant hears.'"
> Then the Lord came and stood and
> called as at the other times.
> 1 Samuel 3:8-10 NKJV

Even children can experience the manifest presence of the Lord. Samuel was so young that he didn't understand what was happening to him. He did not yet know the Lord or the sound of His voice (1 Samuel 3:7). God saw the desire of his heart, came to him, and called him by name.

Samuel had submitted himself to the priest Eli and thought that it was Eli who was calling him. Each time, he rose and went to see what Eli wanted. It was Eli who finally realized that God was speaking to the child.

This experience totally changed Samuel's life. Very early he became aware of God's presence with him and learned how to commune with God and to hear His voice. The lifestyle he developed made him a powerful prophet. During a period when the prophetic word of God was not known, Samuel could boldly speak forth the most profound revelations—because he knew God and heard His voice.

He was a man of God's presence and a man of God's word. The two go together. People of God's presence are also people of His word.

LIGHT

Once, during a worship seminar in Akron, Ohio, a woman came up to me and said that she had seen a very bright light over my shoulder. She thought her eyes were playing tricks on her, so she blinked repeatedly; but the light would not go away. It could very well have been the manifest presence of the Lord.

Saul of Tarsus experienced something similar but much more intense. It was the awesome presence of the Lord as a great light on the road to Damascus. It was the middle of the day, and the sun was probably very bright. Yet a greater light overshadowed the sun and blinded him with its strength.

> Suddenly a light shone around him from heaven.
> Then he fell to the ground, and heard a voice.
> Acts 9:3-4 NKJV

Saul was not a believer, and he certainly was not a worshiper. In fact, he was a persecutor of the church and a murderer, helping to deliver Christians to prison and to death. Yet his encounter with the light of Jesus' presence made him know that He was real. What a miracle of grace that God chose to show the glory of His presence to Saul of Tarsus!

A GREATER LIGHT OVERSHADOWED THE SUN AND BLINDED HIM

> "Saul, Saul, why are you persecuting Me?" And he
> said, "Who are You, Lord?" and the Lord said, "I am
> Jesus, whom you are persecuting."… So he, trembling
> and astonished, said, "Lord, what do You want me
> to do?" And the Lord said to him, "Arise and go into
> the city, and you will be told what you must do."
> Acts 9:4-6 NKJV

The presence of Jesus overwhelmed Saul. When he saw Jesus' glory, he immediately fell down prostrate, trembling with fear. His traveling companions heard a voice but couldn't understand what God was saying. The message was for Saul.

> The men who journeyed with him stood
> speechless, hearing a voice but seeing no one.
> Acts 9:7 NKJV

Apart from the fact that Saul was a rebel, who was capturing and tormenting believers, the interesting point here is that Jesus Himself appeared. This was not an ark or a cloud. Jesus was speaking directly to one of His obstinate enemies.

SOUND AND FIRE

One of the most well known portions of scripture in the New Testament concerning the manifest presence of the Lord is found in the Book of Acts. As the disciples were waiting in the upper room to receive God's power in their lives, God's presence was manifested as a great sound, like wind, and as flames of fire.

WHEN HE SAW JESUS' GLORY, HE IMMEDIATELY FELL DOWN TREMBLING WITH FEAR

Jesus had told them to wait in Jerusalem for "the Promise of the Father." In the scriptures the word "Promise" has a capital "P," because the promise was that God Himself would live in them by His Spirit. He was the Promise.

When they had waited patiently in His presence for ten days, something happened:

> Suddenly there came a sound from heaven, as of a rushing
> mighty wind, and it filled the whole house where they
> were sitting. Then there appeared to them divided tongues,
> as of fire, and one sat upon each of them. And they
> were all filled with the Holy Spirit and began to speak
> with other tongues, as the Spirit gave them utterance.
> Acts 2:2-4 NKJV

I find several things about their experience very intriguing. First, it was obvious to the disciples that the sound they heard came from heaven and was not caused by some natural phenomena. The only thing they could liken it to was a "rushing, mighty wind." It must have been like what audio technicians call white noise—many frequencies sounding simultaneously. It is the sound of wind, water, and fire.

This sound was like white noise or a very strong wind, but was not. It was a sound from heaven. Not much is known about the sounds in heaven, but John the Revelator was able to overhear some of them.

> I heard a voice from heaven, like the voice of many
> waters and like the voice of loud thunder. And I

> heard the sound of harpists playing their harps. And
> they sang as it were a new song before the throne.
> Revelation 14:2-3 NKJV

John described what he heard as "the voice of many waters." This must have been the white noise of heaven.

> I heard, as it were, the voice of a great multitude,
> as the sound of many waters and as the sound
> of mighty thunderings, saying, "Alleluia! For
> the Lord God Omnipotent reigns!"
> Revelation 19:6 NKJV

Perhaps what John heard was the same sound heard in the upper room on the Day of Pentecost.

Secondly, those present in the upper room witnessed flames of fire. Divided flames rested on each of the disciples. God was with them. Everyone knew it. The presence of the Lord was both heard and seen that day.

As a result of this supernatural presence of God, the disciples were filled with the Holy Spirit and began to speak in other languages. When the noise of the disciples' joyful praise was heard in the streets of the city, a large crowd began to gather. The presence of the Lord had an impact on the disciples and, through them, upon the whole city of Jerusalem.

As we have seen so far, the presence of God manifests in many different ways. At times it is so heavy that we feel overwhelmed by Him and must bow our faces to the earth. Other times He is revealed as a voice that rocks our world. And God also manifests as light so brilliant that no one can look upon it. We hide our faces. God determines His appearance depending on the needs of each encounter with Him.

CHAPTER THIRTEEN
STUDY GUIDE

SCRIPTURE

Read Acts 2 and Acts 9.

QUESTIONS

1. Why did Jonah run from the manifest presence of God?

2. What was Samuel's response when confronted by the presence of God?

3. What happened when Jesus revealed His presence to Saul?

4. What different forms did the manifest presence of God take?

5. How did these forms impact or affect those that experienced them?

6. What is the significance and meaning of "the sound of a rushing wind?"

REFLECTION

1. What form of God's manifest presence intrigues you and why?

2. Have you seen the manifest presence of God revealed in a certain way?

3. What is the Holy Spirit saying to you through this chapter?

PRAYER / CONFESSION

Heavenly Father,

You manifest your presence in so many different ways. You know perfectly how to reveal your essence for every need.

Thank you for revealing your presence to me in the way I need to know You and experience You. Make me aware of your presence especially when I need to know You are near.

In Jesus Name,

Amen

MEDITATE / MEMORIZE

> Suddenly a light shone around him from heaven.
> Then he fell to the ground, and heard a voice.
> Acts 9:3-4 NKJV

14

IMMANUEL

The sun began to set as Joseph finished his chores—feeding his donkey and ensuring everything was as it should be for the night. Then he prepared himself for bed and lied down on his straw mattress. He pulled the horse hair blanket over his shoulders and contemplated the events of the day.

These last few days had been challenging for Joseph. He was engaged to a beautiful young girl named Mary whom he loved dearly. She was a virtuous woman and deeply devout. However, she had just told him she was pregnant. Joseph was shocked!

They were not married but as a Jew their ten-month engagement period was taken very seriously. Unfaithfulness during the engagement period would be considered adultery.

What bothered Joseph was he knew the child wasn't his. His fifteen-year-old fiancé said an angel told her this was a supernatural pregnancy. How was he supposed to think about all of this?

The anxiety of what to do about the situation troubled Joseph. He was contemplating a discrete divorce from their engagement. Mary had said she was pregnant by the Holy Spirit. He had never heard of someone being pregnant by the Spirit of God. Joseph was not convinced this would turn out well. With those thoughts running through his mind, he drifted off to sleep.

> **JOSEPH LOWERED...HIS EYES, NOT WANTING TO LOOK AT THE DIVINE CREATURE**

Without warning a very bright light filled the room. Joseph looked up holding his right arm over his forehead, trying to see what the source was. His eyes had a hard time adjusting to the brightness of the light. Then he heard a deep, masculine voice say, "Joseph, descendent of David, don't be concerned about taking Mary as your wife. What has happened to her is from God. The child conceived in her is from the Spirit of God."

Joseph realized that it was an angel who was standing in front of him. His jaw dropped. Joseph lowered his arm and eyes, not wanting to look at the divine creature out of reverence. The room was filled with a heavenly presence.

The shining celestial spoke again, "Mary will give birth to a son, and you will name Him Jesus."

A few hours later Joseph awoke and realized what had occurred was a dream. He sat there for a while on his bed and replayed it in his head. Mary is pregnant by the Holy Spirit, and I should not hesitate to marry her. She will have a son, and I am to name Him Jesus, though others will call Him Immanuel, "God with us."

From that moment on Joseph knew that the child he was to raise would be "God-who-came-to-us-and-dwelled-among-us." He went to tell

Mary. He gave her a warm embrace and told her about his dream. He recommitted himself to marry her and raise the child. Joseph knew God was doing something very special and that He was with them.

GOD WITH US

God's promise of companionship is revealed in the name "Immanuel," which means "God is with us." The rich revelation given to Isaiah of the presence of God with His people included this specific name.

HE PROMISES TO ALWAYS BE WITH YOU

> Therefore the Lord himself shall give you a
> sign; Behold, a virgin shall conceive, and bear
> a son, and shall call his name Immanuel.
> Isaiah 7:14 KJV

Matthew saw Immanuel (or Emmanuel) as the fulfillment of the prophecy of Isaiah—when Jesus came to earth as a man. He quoted Isaiah:

> Behold, a virgin shall be with child, and shall bring
> forth a son, and they shall call his name Emmanuel,
> which being interpreted is, God with us.
> Matthew 1:23 KJV

What a promise! The Almighty Eternal God is with those that believe in Him. His presence was manifested in mortal flesh as Jesus, the Christ child—born of Spirit and revealed in human flesh.

He still makes Himself available today to those who love Him. He is still Immanuel. He is still God with you. You can experience His presence anytime you need to.

He is not only with you (and in you) at the moment you accepted Him as your Lord and Savior, but He also wants to manifest Himself to you often, giving you a constant assurance of His nearness.

ALWAYS NEAR

These promises are never outdated or irrelevant to our daily lives. They are just as true today as they were in David's time. God is just as much present to deliver you from your giants as He was to deliver the young David from Goliath.

Jesus included a promise of His abiding presence with the great commission He gave to His disciples before He left them.

> Go ye therefore, and teach all nations, baptizing them
> in the name of the Father, and of the Son, and of
> the Holy Ghost: Teaching them to observe all things
> whatsoever I have commanded you: and, lo, I am with
> you always, even unto the end of the world. Amen
> Matthew 28:20 KJV

The Lord of the harvest will be with us, not only in His omnipresent sense but also in a real sense. Then, when the age is finished, we will be with Him forever. Throughout eternity, our knowledge of God will increase, and we will encounter Him in a much greater way.

> For now we see through a glass, darkly; but
> then face-to-face: now I know in part; but then
> shall I know even as also I am known.
> 1 Corinthians 13:12 KJV

We have a promise we will know the Lord in a much more intimate way. We will understand what Moses experienced when he saw God face to face. No matter how glorious the dimension of His manifest presence has been to us here on the earth, greater awareness of Him awaits us—in His ultimate presence.

In the meantime you have the assurance that He is with you at every moment of every day, and that you have nothing to fear. Believe His promise to be with you. As you go forth to make His name known, He promises to always be with you. He will never forsake you. This is the promise of His manifest presence, if you seek to encounter Him.

CHAPTER FOURTEEN
STUDY GUIDE

SCRIPTURE

Read Isaiah 7 and Matthew 1.

QUESTIONS

1. What impacted you the most about Joseph's dream?

2. How did God reveal his manifest presence to mankind as Immanuel?

3. What does the name Immanuel mean?

4. How is Jesus a revelation of God's presence?

5. How do we know that God will be with us always?

6. When we go to other places and make disciples, will God be with us, and how do we know?

REFLECTION

1. What is significant or meaningful to you about Jesus as Immanuel?

2. What will you change in your approach to life knowing God wants to be with you in all that you do?

3. What is the Holy Spirit saying to you through this chapter?

PRAYER / CONFESSION

Heavenly Father,

I acknowledge that you are my Immanuel and that means you are always with me. I know I can experience your manifest presence no matter where I am.

May the abiding presence of Your Holy Spirit be real and tangible to me as a reminder that you are constantly near. I realize that your presence is truly with me.

In Jesus Name,

Amen.

MEDITATE / MEMORIZE

Behold, a virgin shall be with child, and shall bring
forth a son, and they shall call his name Emmanuel,
which being interpreted is, God with us.
Matthew 1:23 KJV

CHAPTER FIFTEEN
PROMISE

○──○

The judge's hammer fell with a loud bang, and then those violent words pierced the atmosphere, "Guilty as charged!"

The single mother dropped her head in her hands and wept. The tears rolled down her wrist and across the handcuffs that bond her. "How can this be possible?" She said to herself. "I am innocent. I didn't do what they accuse me of!"

Yet, the jury had found her guilty. "I don't understand!"

"What will happen to my children? Will I see them again?"

These thoughts ran violently through her mind, demolishing all that she believed and hoped for. That is when she distinctly heard the voice, "Do not fear! I am with you!"

The clarity of the voice shook to her core. It voice was so strong, persuasive and personal. She looked around and discerned the voice was heavenly. She received it as a word from the Lord, and an hour later walked peacefully into her cell and into her "new normal."

The metal cell door forcefully slammed behind her.

GOD'S WILLINGNESS TO LOWER HIMSELF TO OUR LEVEL AND TO PERSONALLY ACCOMPANY US ON OUR PILGRIMAGE THROUGH LIFE

ASSURANCE

The Word of God is full of assurances that God will be with you, just like he told this single mother. Although He is always with everyone everywhere, He has promised to show us, or reveal, His presence to each one of us.

These are the most precious promises of the Bible, for they declare God's willingness to lower Himself to our level and to personally accompany us on our pilgrimage through life.

How privileged we are! While the world around us is filled with a terrible sense of loneliness and fear, you never need to be without the presence of your Protector and Provider. This is certainly a lesson that every Christian should learn, for too many have grown accustomed to living without God's personal touch in their daily lives.

GOD SPEAKS

The promise of the Lord's presence is both collective (for us all as God's people) and personal. The Word of God speaks to us as a group as He did to Israel:

> As the mountains are round about Jerusalem, so the Lord
> is round about his people from henceforth even forever.
> Psalms 125:2 KJV

> Then Haggai, the messenger of the Lord, spoke
> by the commission of the Lord to the people
> saying, "'I am with you,' declares the LORD."
> Haggai 1:13 NASB

The Word of God also carries many promises of His presence that speak to us as individuals.

When Isaac was forced to leave his lands and go to Beersheba because of his contentious neighbors, the Lord appeared to him that night and assured him:

> Fear not, for I am with thee.
> Genesis 26:24 KJV

Also, God promised Moses that he would not walk alone when he went back to Egypt to confront the evil Pharaoh. The God of the universe would go with him and help him every step of the way.

> Certainly, I will be with you.
> Exodus 3:12 KJV

Then when Moses died, God promised Joshua that He would accompany him, as He had Moses.

Dozens of average men in the Bible received similar promises and did great things for the Lord. It is one of the great aspects of God's story—He comes to help mortal man.

When faced with the challenge of rebuilding the temple, after the return of the exiles, in the days of the prophet Haggai, God spoke very clearly to those in charge:

> "'But now take courage, Zerubbabel,' declares the
> Lord, 'take courage also, Joshua son of Jehozadak,
> the high priest, and all you people of the land
> take courage,' declares the Lord, 'and work; for
> I am with you,' declares the Lord of hosts."
> Haggai 2:4 NASB

The same promises are recorded for your encouragement. God is with you, whatever your particular situation in life.

Often, God manifests His presence to us in times of danger or trouble.

> "'Do not fear the king of Babylon anymore,'
> says the Lord. 'For I am with you and will save
> you and rescue you from his power.'"
> Jeremiah 42:11 NLT

And when God does manifest His presence, the situation changes. This promise not only assures that God is with us but that miracles would result as well.

> For the Lord your God is in your midst, the Mighty One,
> who will save. …I will deal with all who afflict you.
> Zephaniah 3:17, 19 NKJV

Nothing could give you more comfort and encouragement than to read and believe the promises of God's manifest presence with His people.

Our cry to God must be, as David said:

> Be not far from me; for trouble is near.
> Psalms 22:11 KJV

These promises were not just for Jeremiah, David and Zerubbabel. They are for every believer to encounter. God is with you to help you with all of life's trials. He wants to be there for you.

YOUR PROMISE

God has promised to accompany you on your journey of life, freely giving you the benefits of His fellowship, His care, His provision and His strength.

God is your fortress. In Him, you find safety. He is your protection, your sanctuary—not in an ethereal or abstract sense, but in reality. This is not a theological concept. This is a tangible blessing.

God is your rest in the midst of the turmoil of life. He is with you in battle. He goes before you to utter His voice before His army. When you go to war against evil and unclean spirits, He is always present to preserve and protect those He loves.

When Judah had to go out to war against backslidden Israel, Abijah comforted and encouraged the people with these powerful words:

God himself is with us for our captain.
2 Chronicles 13:12 KJV

When the Assyrians, under the famous Sennacherib, invaded Judah and threatened to destroy the city of Jerusalem, Hezekiah took courage and spoke to his captains:

HE IS ALWAYS PRESENT TO PRESERVE AND PROTECT THOSE HE LOVES

With us is the Lord our God.
2 Chronicles 32:8 KJV

In both cases, Judah miraculously prevailed in battle. How could they lose when God was on their side?

We are so precious to the Lord that He uses the most intimate terms of endearment when speaking of us in His Word.

I am with thee. ... For I the Lord thy
God will hold thy right hand...
Isaiah 41:10, 13 KJV

Paul also knew this nurturing of an ever-present and caring God. He said,

The Lord stood with me, and strengthened me.
2 Timothy 4:17 KJV

The Lord of heaven and earth is with us, not only to preserve us, but also to display His power on our behalf. He is with us as Guide, to direct our steps. He is with us as Counselor, to instruct us. He is with us as Friend, to comfort our hearts. And He is with us as Savior, to free us from sin.

This promise of God's presence is the predominant theme of scripture. This is the purpose of God. He has always manifested His presence to His people, and He always will.

The promises of Divine presence with us should bring tremendous stability and strength to every Christian. Earthly friends fail us, but God is faithful. His presence is constant. He doesn't change His mind, break His promise, or withdraw from us—as others may.

Being deprived of human companionship often brings loneliness. The loss of a spouse, or a child, or a close friend is among the most serious emotional trauma that we face in life. The Lord God of heaven and earth says to all those who are lonely:

> I will never leave you, nor forsake you.
> Hebrews 13:5 KJV

Life has its difficult moments for each of us. This is not an easy journey on which we have embarked. But the promise of God's presence with us makes it all worthwhile. He is with us everywhere and always, by His omnipresence. And He has promised to manifest His presence to us in a real and tangible way. We are blessed with a double portion of His presence in our lives.

Others may forsake us, but there is always Someone who is willing to accompany us, to make us recipients of His fellowship, His care, His provision, and His strength.

PERPETUAL

This promise of God's presence with His children has longevity. He has promised to be with us unto the end of the age or unto the end of the world. No matter when we are in need of Him, no matter how often or how long, He is there for us.

Even in complete darkness, He is there to light the way. If the darkness is the shadow of death, He is present to hold and comfort us.

> Even though I walk through the valley of the
> shadow of death, I fear no evil, for You are with
> me; Your rod and Your staff, they comfort me.
> Psalms 23:4 NASB

There is nothing more certain in a Christian's life than the promise of God's presence. He never fails. He will perform His Word.

You are favored with such an illustrious presence! Such promises should release you from fear and loneliness and should empower you to witness. The many benefits that the assurance of His presence gives you should motivate you to take time to cultivate His presence in your daily lives.

CHAPTER FIFTEEN
STUDY GUIDE

SCRIPTURE

Read Exodus 3 and Psalms 23.

QUESTIONS

1. What did God promise Isaac and Moses?

2. In what situations does God often manifest his presence

3. Name three promises God has given us about His presence?

4. How is God's revealed presence a predominant theme in the Bible?

5. What happens when God is with us in spiritual conflict?

6. How can we know God will be with us in any situation?

REFLECTION

1. What is it about God's promise of His presence that means the most to you?

2. God promises to be with you not only for a while but forever. How does that encourage you?

3. What is the Holy Spirit saying to you through this chapter?

PRAYER / CONFESSION

Heavenly Father,

I believe that you are with me as you promised in your Word. No matter the circumstance I acknowledge your presence is present to protect and provide. I desire to walk through this day and every day with the awareness that you are very close to me. You have promised that You will never leave me or abandon me.

Thank you so much for the assurance of your nearness and care.

In Jesus name,

Amen

MEDITATE / MEMORIZE

Even though I walk through the valley of the
shadow of death, I fear no evil, for You are with
me; Your rod and Your staff, they comfort me.
Psalms 23:4 NASB

ENCOUNTERS

The Lord would speak to Moses face to
face, as one speaks to a friend
Exodus 33:11 NLT

16

CHAPTER SIXTEEN
ENOCH

○──○

It was late afternoon, almost dusk, in the Fertile Crescent where Enoch lived. It was the time when he would meet with God. Enoch enjoyed these regular encounters. They were what he lived for.

This day God came in a formless mist ever swirling and moving. It was their routine to stroll together, conversing about the eternal realm of Yahweh's kingdom. Enoch was over three hundred years old and had been meeting with God for several centuries.

During these divine encounters God revealed insights and understanding of the spiritual world. The dialog enriched Enoch's understanding of the kingdom of heaven. God shared with him the mystery of the ranks and activities of angels and demons, including insights into Satan and the kingdom of darkness.

Like a scholar, Enoch wrote down what God told him after each encounter. He recorded what God said about the fallen angels and how they corrupted the human race by having sexual relations with mortal women.

Like Adam, six generations prior, Enoch had the privilege of encountering God's revealed presence and visiting with Him. Enoch walked and talked with God just as Adam had.

INTIMATE ENCOUNTERS WITH GOD'S MANIFEST PRESENCE PRODUCE SOLID FAITH

…Enoch lived in close fellowship with God for another 300 years… Enoch lived 365 years, walking in close fellowship with God. Then one day he disappeared, because God took him.
Genesis 5:22–24 NLT

Enoch was the son of Jared, a descendant of Adam through Seth. He is better known as the father of Methuselah (the oldest man in the Bible). Enoch, like Elisha, did not taste death. God took him away after communing with Him three hundred years.

The word "walked" in Genesis 5 is intriguing. It means the going, movement, or way of man, like the creeping of a snake, or the prowling of foxes, or the flowing of water. It could mean the procession of man or, in a general sense, the journey of man through life. It speaks of the continuity of action or movement. Enoch lived his life in a continuum of communion with God.

Enoch strolled with God and was close to Him. Enoch knew the manifest presence of God in his life. The two of them, Enoch and God, walked together. They had sweet communion and intimate fellowship with each other. They had a cherished friendship. Enoch lived in the manifest presence of the Lord.

It was because of his faith that Enoch was taken up and did not have to experience death: he was not to be found because God had taken him.
Hebrews 11:5 The Jerusalem Bible

Another translation says that he was taken up to God, or to heaven. All this happened because of Enoch's faith in what God said.

As Christians, we must have faith in God and in what He has spoken. This is the faith that gives substance to the things we hope for and certainty to the things we don't yet see.

As Enoch and God walked, they conversed with each other. Enoch talked with God, and God talked with Enoch. When God told him something, Enoch believed it.

Intimate encounters with God's manifest presence produce solid faith and strong confidence. Enoch had strong faith because he communed with God constantly. He believed God because he knew Him intimately.

We don't know all that God told Enoch. Did He tell him that he would not die? Perhaps. But whatever God said to him, Enoch believed. And because he believed, he experienced what God had promised him.

> It was because of his faith that Enoch was taken to
> the eternal world without experiencing death.
> Hebrews 11:5 Phillips

Enoch was "translated." God picked him up and carried him away to the eternal realm. In that encounter, Enoch experienced God's manifest presence in a very special way.

The challenge we receive from the life of Enoch is twofold: to walk with God and to believe what He says. To walk with God is to spend time in His presence, to live in a constant state of God-consciousness. To walk with God is to commune and fellowship with Him on a regular basis, to be where He is and to get to know Him.

To walk by faith is to be motivated, not by the circumstances around us, but by what God says.

Perhaps you have experienced being caught up into a higher dimension, in which you were totally oblivious to the natural realm. For a while, you lost all awareness of time and space, so that hours in His presence seemed like only a few minutes.

Do you long to experience that kind of encounter? Let Enoch's life be an example to you of a higher dimension of encountering God. Seek to commune and converse with Him passionately and intimately. Let it be your way of living. Then it may be said of you, "(Insert your name here) walked with God."

CHAPTER SIXTEEN
STUDY GUIDE

SCRIPTURE

Read Genesis 5.

QUESTIONS

1. Who was Enoch?

2. How did Enoch experience the manifest presence of God?

3. What was unique about Enoch and his relationship with God?

4. What does it mean to "walk with God" as Enoch did?

5. What happened to Enoch that was very unusual?

6. How does Enoch's life challenge us?

7. What role does faith have in encountering God?

REFLECTION

1. What strikes you about Enoch's relationship with God?

2. After reading this chapter what would you change to encounter God's presence like Enoch did?

3. What is the Holy Spirit saying to you through this chapter?

PRAYER / CONFESSION

Heavenly Father,

I desire to walk with You as Enoch did. To commune and talk with You as a course of life is pray.

I pray that is may it be said of me that I walked with God.

In Jesus name,

Amen

MEDITATE / MEMORIZE

> ...Enoch lived in close fellowship with God
> for another 300 years... Enoch lived 365 years,
> walking in close fellowship with God. Then one
> day he disappeared, because God took him.
> Genesis 5:22–24 NLT

17

ABRAHAM

The nomadic Aramean signaled to his servants, pointing to the ground under his feet.

"Here," he said. The servants bowed and quickly dispersed to set up camp.

This was one of the most significant spots the patriarch Abraham had visited. This place was Mamre, quickly identifiable by the giant oak trees that grew there providing ample shade for the meandering Bedouin.

When his tent was pitched, Abraham reclined at the entrance leaning on his elbow. It was cooler outside the tent. The heat that summer was very intense, but outside his tent he could feel a gentle breeze.

Abraham's mind wandered thinking of the favor God had shown him by leading him to this land. He glanced up at the large trees in front of him and then suddenly noticed three strangers standing together at the top of the hill looking at him.

Abraham quickly jumped up and briskly walked toward the men. Each of them were tall with a dark complexion and a celestial countenance.

ABRAHAM WOULD SOON FIND OUT THAT THESE THREE MEN WERE GOD

Abraham would soon find out that these three men were God.

CHOSEN

The name Abraham, means father of a multitude. God gave it to Abram (a descendant of Shem). Abraham is revered as the father of all Jews and Christians and the first of the great patriarchs.

God chose Abraham as the man through whom He wanted to bless all mankind and called him to a unique walk of faith. Abraham would leave his own land and his father's family and travel toward a new land, which God would show him. In that new place God would raise up, from Abraham's loins, a new nation to serve Him.

> The Lord had said to Abram, "Leave your country,
> your people and your father's household and
> go the land I will show you. I will make you
> into a great nation and I will bless you."
> Genesis 12:1–2 NIV

But to get to this new place, Abraham would need to cross three hundred miles of hostile territory. And once he arrived in Canaan, he would wander with his family for many years as a nomad, in search of food and water for his many flocks.

As a foreigner, Abraham was not permitted to own land or to build a permanent dwelling, very difficult for a man who was accustomed to prosperity in his homeland. His willingness to obey God in these difficult circumstances has been an example of faith. Abraham trusted God deeply.

> And the Scripture was fulfilled that says, "Abraham
> believed God, and it was counted to him as
> righteousness"—and he was called a friend of God.
> James 2:23 ESV

Abraham believed God. He had total confidence and assurance in Him. Because of that, they were friends. You see friends trust each other. There is a bond that keeps them as friends.

TRUST

Abraham's unquestioning faith and trust was a result of his intimate relationship with God. He and God often had conversations. Because they were close, God could trust Abraham with His plan.

> So Abram left, as the Lord had told him. ...
> The Lord appeared to Abram and said, "To your
> offspring I will give this land." So he built an altar
> there to the Lord, who had appeared to him.
> Genesis 12:4, 7 NIV

At every juncture of his life, God was there to say to Abraham just what he needed to hear at the moment. His intimate relationship with God guided him through life and the decisions he had to make.

> The Lord appeared to him and said, "I am
> God Almighty, walk before me and be
> blameless." ... Abram fell facedown.
> Genesis 17:1, 3 NIV

God's presence revealed to Abraham was awe-inspiring. Sometimes God appeared to Abraham in visions (Genesis 15:1–3). Sometimes Abraham heard the audible voice of God (verses 13 & 18), and sometimes the manifestation of God's presence to Abraham was very unusual.

> The Lord said to him, "Bring me a heifer, a goat and
> a ram, each three years old, along with a dove and a
> young pigeon." Abraham brought all these to him, cut

> them in two and arranged the halves opposite each
> other; the birds, however, he did not cut in half.
> ...As the sun was setting, Abram fell into a deep sleep,
> and a thick and dreadful darkness came over him.
> ...When the sun had set and darkness had fallen,
> a smoking firepot with a blazing torch appeared
> and passed between the pieces. On that day
> the Lord made a covenant with Abram.
> Genesis 15:9–10, 12, 17–18 NIV

As Abraham slept, a dark, heavy cloud of blackness came over him. This could very possibly have been a manifestation of the presence of God. Then a pot of fire and smoke and a blazing torch moved between the pieces of the sacrifice Abraham had made. It is possible that the fiery pot and the torch were manifestations of God's presence in confirma¬tion of the pact He and Abraham were making.

VISITORS

> The Lord appeared to Abraham near the great trees
> of Mamre while he was sitting at the entrance to
> his tent in the heat of the day. Abraham looked
> up and saw three men standing nearby. When he
> saw them, he hurried from the entrance of his tent
> to meet them and bowed low to the ground.
> Genesis 18:1–2 NIV

On this occasion, God appeared to Abraham as a human visitor, a very unusual manifestation of His presence. With Him were two angels, also in human form. It is not clear whether Abraham immediately recognized that he was talking with God. But very quickly the nature of his visitors became evident. This visitor knew the name of Abraham's wife and knew the fact that she was barren.

> Then the Lord said, "I will surely return to you about this
> time next year, and Sarah your wife will have a son."
> Genesis 18:10 NIV

Abraham's Visitor was God Himself. The Scriptures call Him "the Lord," and what He proposed was clearly impossible—in human terms. He said that Sarah would become pregnant, when she was already too old to have children.

God could have sent an angel to speak with Abraham. He could have given him a dream or a vision. He could have sent a prophet. On this occasion, however, He decided to take the message personally and appeared to Abraham as a man.

ON THIS OCCASSION GOD APPEARED TO ABRAHAM AS A HUMAN VISITOR

Many people have seen God and talked to God in visions. But Abraham had the privilege of sitting down with God around a Bedouin table and having a conversation over lunch. This is the blessing of friendship— friends have frank conversations with each other in intimate settings.

God ate a meal with Abraham—an expression of intimacy. They conversed and broke bread together as friends, enjoying each other's presence in a very tangible and friendly way.

SODOM

When the men got up to leave, they looked down toward Sodom, and Abraham walked along with them to see them on their way. Then the Lord said, "Shall I hide from Abraham what I am about to do?"

> ...Then the Lord said, "The outcry of Sodom and
> Gomorrah is so great and their sin so grievous that I
> will go down and see if what they have done is as bad
> as the outcry that has reached me. If not I will know."
> Genesis 18:16–17, 20–21 NIV

The Lord wanted to "go down" to Sodom. You might say that He wanted to personally check out the extent of the perversion that was reported to be there. His omnipresence is everywhere. He monitors everything, and He knows everything. Here, however, He indicated a desire to have a closer look. God was about to go down, and convince Himself of whether they had done according to the cry which had reached Him or not. This was an indication that He wanted to reveal Himself among the filth, lewdness, and obscenity of Sodom and Gomorrah.

> The men turned away and went toward Sodom,
> but Abraham remained standing before the
> Lord. Then Abraham approached him.
> Genesis 18:22–23 NIV

God told Abraham about the sin of Sodom and Gomorrah and what He intended to do with the people there because He knew that Abraham was a man of intercession, and Abraham interceded for the inhabitants of those two cities.

The two men, or angels, went to Sodom. There they accepted the hospitality of Lot and the protection of his home. When the depraved men of Sodom knew that Lot had guests (and these angels must have been tall, good-looking men), they demanded that he release them, presuming them to be normal men whom they could abuse.

The inhabitants of Sodom had become so morally depraved and under the influence of unclean spirits that its men disregarded their work and relationships and were obsessed with abusing these visitors. The men didn't ask Lot if they could speak to his guests. They demanded that he release them into their hands. What shameless lust and compulsive addiction! These men burned with insatiable desire to fulfill their sexual fantasies without any consideration for others. Every age group and every class of person was in the crowd unashamedly crying out for these very handsome and masculine men from heaven.

God saw that the insatiable desires of the residents of Sodom to rape and abuse whomever they wanted could not even be abated by the presence of his angels. It was so serious that God manifested His presence to see the situation. In someway, perhaps, He desired that His presence would either convict or convince them or Abraham.

LOT

Lot did not consent to the demands of the crowd, but he was powerless to stop them. However, God was ready to reveal Himself to the inhabitants of Sodom. He went there so they could encounter His presence and know Him, but the people of Sodom were totally intoxicated by their lust. God is willing to manifest His presence anywhere, to anyone, when there is the possibility that men and women may turn to Him.

The angels had to grab Lot and pull him back into his house because his neighbors were attempting to physically drag him away. The crowd was not happy with the action of the visitors. Like raging beasts they attempted to tear down the door of the house to get to their prey. To prevent further violence, the angels struck the men blind so that they were unable to find the door.

God had offered to reveal His presence and mercy to the people of Sodom. However, that they had reacted in such a contemptible manner only proved the inevitable: Sodom must be destroyed. The angels said:

> "The outcry to the Lord against its people is
> so great that he has sent us to destroy it."
> Genesis 19:13 NIV

And soon the destruction of the city began.

> Then the Lord rained down burning sulfur on Sodom
> and Gomorrah— from the Lord out of the heavens.
> Genesis 19:24 NIV

Unless God's presence among sinners produces repentance and confession of sin, the final outcome will always be judgment. The burning sulfur came from the Lord Himself—His very presence.

Do you see the contrast in this chapter between a man who is a friend of God—enjoying God's fellowship and conversation—and flagrant, shameless sex addicts who reject God's presence and would rather rape than encounter God's manifest presence? What a distinction! It bears the question where are our strongest affections directed?

CHAPTER SEVENTEEN
STUDY GUIDE

SCRIPTURE

Read Genesis 18 and 19.

QUESTIONS

1. What does the name Abraham mean?

2. Why do you think Abraham was called a friend of God?

3. How did Abraham acquire his strong faith in God?

4. God revealed Himself to Abraham several times and on one occasion conversed with him while eating a meal. What does that tell us about God?

5. What is the importance of the phrasing when God said that He wanted to "go down" to Sodom?

6. How did the people of Sodom encounter God's presence?

REFLECTION

1. How are you impacted by Abraham's friendship and closeness to God?

2. What speaks to you in this chapter, seeing the contrast between a man who wants to intimately encounter God and sinners who refuse to?

3. What is the Holy Spirit saying to you through this chapter?

PRAYER / CONFESSION

Heavenly Father,

Abraham's friendship with you inspires me to desire to get closer to you. I want to be a friend of yours. Your kindness and affection for me leads me to want to be more connected with you.

I commit to pursue your intimate presence. Thank you for your loving friendship.

In Jesus Name,

Amen

MEDITATE / MEMORIZE

And the Scripture was fulfilled that says, "Abraham believed God, and it was counted to him as righteousness"—and he was called a friend of God.
James 2:23 ESV

18

JACOB

○———————————————————————————————————○

The sun was setting behind the hills, casting a pearlescent glow across the valley. Jacob had a strong sense that he should camp here for the night. He started a fire and made himself a bed. Gathering grass and leaves he laid them on a level patch of ground. Then he selected a stone for his pillow and laid one of his animal skin bottles on it.

After a few minutes he lay down on his makeshift bed. Fatigued by the long journey and saddened by thoughts of the family he had left behind, he fell into a deep sleep. It was then that he had the most unusual dream.

He saw a flight of steps, a rock stairway, leading from the ground into heaven. The dream was extraordinary not only because the stairway reached into the third heaven but also because he saw angelic beings going up and down on the steps. They glowed with a golden brilliance and shone into the darkness that was at the bottom of the stairway.

The celestials seemed very focused on the purpose of their ascent and descent, not noticing what was beside or below them. Their attention was on the object at the top of the stairs. There stood Jehovah—the Supreme Ruler of heaven and earth. Jehovah was standing. Jacob was lying, but his God was standing—presiding over and protecting Jacob. When he saw Jehovah, he had this incredible sense that the ever-surveying presence of God was watching over him.

Immediately Jacob heard the Lord say,

> "I am the Lord, the God of your grandfather
> Abraham, and the God of your father, Isaac.
> The ground you are lying on belongs to you. I
> am giving it to you and your descendants."

> "I am with you and will watch over you wherever you
> go, and I will bring you back to this land. I will not
> leave you until I have done what I have promised you."

> When Jacob awoke from his sleep, he thought, "Surely the
> Lord is in this place, and I was not aware of it." He was
> afraid and said, "How awesome is this place! This is none
> other than the house of God; this is the gate of heaven."
> Genesis 28:12–13, 15–17 NLT & NIV

Then Jacob sat up and looked around, quickly recognizing that his vision was a dream. He had witnessed a spiritual portal, an opening to the very presence of God, a stairway with one end touching earth and the other extending into heaven.

Angels were going up the ladder into the presence of God and coming down the ladder from the presence of God. They were entering and exiting God's presence, bringing the glory of His revealed presence with them. Jacob called the place where he encountered the presence of God "the gate of heaven."

BETHEL

Few people have ever seen what Jacob saw that day, the entrance to heaven. Many have seen the Lord and many have seen angels. But few have seen them in this way. What he saw left Jacob in awe. He said, "Surely the Lord is in this place, and I was not aware of it." Jacob, the son of Isaac, the son of Abraham, had experienced the manifest presence of God that Abraham experienced.

JACOB CALLED THE PLACE... "THE GATE OF HEAVEN"

Early the next morning Jacob took the stone he had placed under his head and set it up as a pillar and poured oil on top of it. He called that place Bethel.

> Then Jacob made a vow, saying "...This stone that
> I have set up as a pillar will be God's house."
> Genesis 28:18–22 NIV

Jacob called that place Bethel, meaning "house of God." He had never seen God in this way before. He had never experienced His presence so strongly. Surely God must live in this place. This must be His house—Bethel.

The strange thing about this encounter is that Jacob was not seeking God. He was on a journey to seek a wife. But God was seeking Jacob. He had chosen him to continue the godly line, to pass on the faith of his fathers, Abraham and Isaac, and to become Israel, the nation God had ordained through Abram.

The encounter with God frightened Jacob. He was not totally comfortable in the presence of God. But he made a vow that day: if God would help him on his journey and would allow him to return safely, he would serve Him.

PENIEL

Many years would pass before Jacob returned to his own land. During that time, he lived with his uncle Laban and served him for seven years in order to marry his daughters. By the time he returned to his homeland, he had two wives, eleven sons, and a great herd of cattle. As he camped one night along the way, he had another strange experience, another encounter with God.

> So Jacob was left alone, and a Man wrestled with him
> till daybreak. When the Man saw that He could not
> overpower him, He touched the socket of Jacob's hip so
> that his hip was wrenched as he wrestled with the Man.
> Then the Man said, "Let Me go, for it is daybreak."
> But Jacob replied, "I will not let you
> go unless you bless me."
> The Man asked him, "What is your name?"
> "Jacob," he answered.
> Then the Man said, "Your name will no longer
> be Jacob, but Israel, because you have struggled
> with God and with men and have overcome."
> Then He blessed him there.
> So Jacob called the place Peniel, saying, "It is because
> I saw God face to face, and yet my life was spared."
> Genesis 32:24–28, 29–30 NIV

The passage raises many questions, among them: Who was this man? Was this the Lord God Jehovah? Or was this the pre-incarnate Logos, Jesus, the Christ? If it was the presence of God, why could He not overpower Jacob? Why did the Man say, "let Me go?" Why couldn't He break away from Jacob?

We do not know the exact answer to these questions. What is certain is that Jacob had met with God. The name "Peniel" means "face of God." Jacob knew that he had wrestled with God Himself, had been face to face in a most intimate encounter with Him, and he would never be the same again. He was changed for life. His body was permanently marked where the Lord had touched him—probably limping for the rest of his life.

The sun rose above him as he passed Peniel, and he
was limping because of his hip. Therefore to this
day the Israelites do not eat the tendon attached
to the socket of the hip, because the socket of
Jacob's hip was touched near the tendon.
Genesis 32:31–32 NIV

Jacob carried a visible mark from being in the presence of God. His was much different from the mark Cain wore, banishing him from God's presence and making him a fugitive on the earth. Jacob's mark was just the opposite. He was marked from God's presence. From

JACOB CARRIED A VISIBLE MARK FROM BEING IN THE PRESENCE OF GOD

that night on Jacob's life was different because Jacob was different. The presence of God so impacted his life that he was changed. God's manifest presence will change you—marking your spirit.

But we all, with open face, beholding… the glory
of the Lord, are changed into the same image from
glory to glory, even as by the Spirit of the Lord.
2 Corinthians 3:18 KJV

Those who encounter the manifest presence of God are changed inside and out.

Most often, seeking God is the path to finding God's presence. However, in the case of Jacob, God visited Him—a rare occurrence. It was a visitation that God purposely initiated. Most of the time we must seek Him, and then He rewards us with His revealed essence.

An encounter with the revealed presence of God will change and transform you. I encourage you to seek His presence today. Go to the place where you like to pray and praise and let it be a gateway to heaven.

CHAPTER EIGHTEEN
STUDY GUIDE

SCRIPTURE

Read Genesis 28 and Genesis 32.

QUESTIONS

1. How did Jacob encounter the manifest presence of God?

2. What did Jacob see?

3. Jacob described the places he encountered God in two ways. What were they?

4. What did Jacob name the spot of his first encounter with God?

5. What does that name mean?

6. Later on, Jacob encountered God in another way. Describe what happened.

7. How was Jacob changed from his encounters with God?

8. We often seek God's presence. What was unique about Jacob's encounters with God?

REFLECTION

1. What about Jacob's encounter with God impacts you?

2. What would you do differently after reading about Jacob's encounters with God's presence?

3. What is the Holy Spirit saying to you through this chapter?

PRAYER / CONFESSION

Heavenly Father,

I am intrigued by the encounter Jacob had with You. I too desire to inimately connect with You.

Help me recognize the moments and places that you are near and not take it for granted. 1

In Jesus Name,

Amen

MEDITATE / MEMORIZE

The sun rose above him as he passed Peniel, and he was limping
because of his hip. Therefore to this day the Israelites do not
eat the tendon attached to the socket of the hip, because
the socket of Jacob's hip was touched near the tendon.

Genesis 32:31–32 NIV

19

MOSES

○————————————————————————————○

The shepherd hummed his favorite melody as the sheep followed his voice through the grasslands just on the outskirts of the desert. It was a desolate place, but there was enough grass and water for the sheep. In the distance he could see the mountains relentlessly pointing upward.

There it was, Mt. Sinai. The shepherd prince paused for a moment to gaze at Sinai's peak and thought to himself, "This was a far cry from the palaces and pyramids of Egypt!"

But it was some forty years since he had beheld the grandeur of the greatest civilization on earth. His life and heart had changed. Now life is simpler and more transcendent in the arena of God's creation, working with God's creatures. He enjoyed the change.

Suddenly, out of the corner of his eye, he saw a flickering fire.

"I didn't know there was anyone out here!"

He walked over to see what was burning and who started the fire. That is when he noticed the thorny acacia shrub burning. It appeared unaffected by the flames. Intrigued the shepherd drew closer to examine the strange phenomenon. The heat was intense keeping the shepherd at a distance.

The flames were coming up out of the center of the bush but they were not the kind of flames he had seen before. Yes, they were similar in color— amber with hues of gold—but they were shaped in the form of a man.

Suddenly the ground shook. An earthquake rolled through the wilderness.

"Moses! Moses!" Startled, the shepherd stumbled back and fell to one knee as the voice roared from the bush like a roll of thunder.

"Here I am." The shepherd said timidly leaning on his staff.

The shepherd knew he was in the presence of a heavenly being. But who was this? His hands and arms began to shake, not because he was over eighty years old, but because he was overwhelmed with the Presence in the shrub. Deep reverential fear passed through his body. He could feel heaviness on his head and shoulders.

Again the voice rumbled, "Come closer! Take your shepherd sandals off for this place where you stand is sacred."

Moses quickly stooped down and removed his sandals. He knew the presence of the celestial creature in the shrub had rendered the ground holy.

"I am the God of your ancestors Abraham, Isaac, and Jacob!" The voice announced.

With those words the shepherd bowed his head, afraid to look at Yahweh. Now he knew it was God Himself. Moses got down on both knees, bowed his head to the ground and worshiped.

That encounter with God marked Moses as a man of God's presence. He would not be satisfied with anything less. His life would forever be changed by God's revealed presence.

MEETING

Without a doubt one of the greatest men of the Bible is Moses, mostly due to the fact that he spent so much time in the presence of God. Ever since his first encounter with God in the bush, Moses loved God's presence and encountered Him often.

THE SHEPHERD BOWED HIS HEAD, AFRAID TO LOOK AT YAHWEH

After he had met God face to face that first time, Moses took advantage of every opportunity to commune with God and experience Him intimately. He talked to God in the glory on Mt. Sinai. He talked to God in the tent of meeting.

> Moses took his tent and pitched it outside the camp,
> far from the camp, and called it the tabernacle
> of meeting. And it came to pass that everyone
> who sought the Lord went out to the tabernacle
> of meeting, which was outside the camp.
> Exodus 33:7 KJV

Moses did whatever was necessary—no effort was too great—so that he and all Israel could seek the Lord. He was not afraid to withdraw himself from the crowd if it was necessary.

If a special tent were necessary, he would make a special tent. The tent that Moses made, "the tent of meeting," became such a blessing to the children of Israel. It turned their lives around.

> So it was, whenever Moses went out to the tabernacle, that
> all the people rose, and each man stood at his tent door
> and watched Moses until he had gone into the tabernacle.
> And it came to pass, when Moses entered the tabernacle,

> that the pillar of cloud descended and stood at the door
> of the tabernacle, and the Lord talked with Moses.
> Exodus 33:8–9 KJV

The people loved to see Moses go to the tent. It was an exciting moment for them. Perhaps in some way, they were expecting to see God display His power.

FRIEND

Moses was God's friend because he spent time in conversation with the Lord. God drew near to Moses, and Moses drew near to God. They had a mutually rewarding relationship. God enjoyed speaking with Moses and enjoyed meeting him at the Ark of the Covenant.

> There I will meet with you, and I will speak with you from
> above the mercy seat, from between the two cherubim,
> which are on the ark of the Testimony, of all things, which
> I will give you in commandment to the children of Israel.
> Exodus 25:22 KJV

God was ready to reveal Himself. He was ready to speak with Moses and to instruct Him. But Moses had to make the effort to approach. He did so because he had a thirst for God's presence. He knew that he could not lead the children of Israel alone. He knew that he was nothing without the Lord's hand, and presence, upon his life.

> Then Moses said to Him, "If Your Presence does not
> go with us, do not bring us up from here. For how
> then will it be known that Your people and I have
> found grace in Your sight, except You go with us?
> So we shall be separate, Your people and I, from all
> the people who are upon the face of the earth."
> Exodus 33:15–16 KJV

DISTINCTION

The presence of God was so important to the children of Israel that Moses wanted them to be known as a people of the Presence. He wanted them to be recognized as different from all other nations—because they had the presence of the Creator of heaven and earth in their midst, because they had a relationship with their God, because they knew His presence.

The gods of the other religions are only idols of men or spiritual principalities. Entering their presence is not pleasant. You would not want to stay long. Their worship is motivated by fear and superstition, not love. God's presence brings rest and peace.

> My Presence will go with you, and I will give you rest.
> Exodus 33:14 KJV

Moses' deep relationship with God was unique. On one occasion Moses spent forty days in the presence of God (Exodus 24:15–18). What do you think it would be like to spend over five consecutive weeks in God's manifest presence?

On another occasion:

> The Lord came down in the pillar of cloud and stood
> in the door of the tabernacle, and called Aaron and
> Miriam. And they both went forward. Then He said,
> "…My servant Moses: He is faithful in all My house.
> I speak with him face to face, even plainly, and not
> in dark sayings; and he sees the form of the Lord
> Numbers 12:5–8 KJV

Moses saw the silhouette of the Lord. It was some sort of form or shape of the revealed presence of God. Not many men have communed that close to God to see His shape.

Moses had a tremendous longing to be near His Creator and Heavenly Father. On one occasion, He said to God, "Please, show me Your glory" (Exodus 33:18).

The Lord responded to his plea:

> "I will make all my goodness pass before you. You cannot
> see My face; for no man shall see Me, and live. Here is
> a place by Me, and you shall stand on the rock. So it
> shall be, while My glory passes by, that I will put you in

the cleft of the rock, and will cover you with My hand
while I pass by. Then I will take away My hand, and
you shall see My back; but My face shall not be seen."
Exodus 33:19–23 KJV

MOSES SPENT FORTY DAYS IN THE PRESENCE OF GOD

The Lord descended in
the cloud and stood with
him there, and proclaimed
the name of the Lord.
And the Lord passed before him.
So Moses made haste and bowed his head
toward the earth, and worshipped.
Exodus 34:5–6, 8 KJV

Because he spent so much time in God's presence, the Bible says of
Moses:

Since then there has not arisen in Israel a prophet
like Moses, whom the Lord knew face to face.
Deuteronomy 34:10 KJV

What an incredible statement about Moses!

Have you been face to face with God? Do you have a passion to
encounter Him? That is His desire for each of us. He is inviting you to
get in His face as a father invites his children to come close—face to face.

JOSHUA

After the death of Moses the servant of the Lord, it came to pass that the
Lord spoke to Joshua the son of Nun, Moses' assistant, saying:

"As I was with Moses, so I will be with you.
I will not leave you nor forsake you.
Do not be afraid, nor be dismayed, for the Lord
your God is with you wherever you go."
Joshua 1:1, 5–6, 9 KJV

Joshua had the privilege of being an apprentice under Moses, the man who lived face to face with God. As Joshua grew in his own personal knowledge of God, gradually the mantle of leadership passed to him. Joshua also loved the presence of God. On at least one occasion, he stayed behind in the presence of God long after Moses had left.

> So the Lord spoke to Moses face to face, as a man
> speaks to his friend. And he would return to the
> camp, but his servant Joshua the son of Nun, a
> young man, did not depart from the tabernacle.
> Exodus 33:11 KJV

There were many times when Moses went up the mountain to meet with God that Joshua was at his side.

> Moses arose with his assistant Joshua, and
> Moses went up to the mountain of God.
> Exodus 24:13 KJV

On this particular occasion, Joshua waited patiently, for many days and nights, as Moses went up further into the cloud of God's manifest presence.

Because he knew God, Joshua became a military genius who brought many victories to Israel. The tactics he employed in conquering the nations of Canaan are still considered classics of military strategies.

After he had distributed the conquered territory among the tribes, Joshua retired from military life to devote himself to strengthening the worship life of his people. He made this decision at a critical time.

Once all their enemies were conquered, most of the people had relaxed their faith and began to stray from the lord who saved them (Joshua 24:23–27).

Let us not relax in our quest until we are safely in the ultimate presence of God, in eternity. Like Moses and Joshua, I encourage you to maintain a passion for the revealed presence of God—searching and seeking, longing and yearning for the God of your salvation.

CHAPTER NINETEEN
STUDY GUIDE

SCRIPTURE

Read Exodus 3.

QUESTIONS

1. What was unique about Moses?

2. How did Moses encounter the presence of God?

3. To what lengths did Moses go to meet with God's revealed presence?

4. Who did Moses mentor who eventually took his place?

5. How did that leader encounter the presence of God?

6. How were these leaders unique in their encounter with God's manifest presence?

REFLECTION

1. How do all the encounters Moses had with God impact you?

2. What will you do differently after reading this chapter?

3. What is the Holy Spirit saying to you through this chapter?

PRAYER / CONFESSION

Heavenly Father,

I am intrigued by how well Moses knew You and the time he spent with You. I too desire to inimately know You, not just your acts, but your ways as Moses did.

I make it my quest to maintain a passion for your revealed presence. I earnestly desire to dwell in your manifest presence and commune with You there.

In Jesus Name,

Amen

MEDITATE / MEMORIZE

Since then there has not arisen in Israel a prophet
like Moses, whom the Lord knew face to face.
Deuteronomy 34:10 KJV

20

CHAPTER TWENTY
DAVID

○───○

David stumbled over the rocky terrain, almost twisting his ankle on a stone. He staggered through the low brush trying to find a place to hide. He surveyed the terrain and found a place to rest for a moment. He let out a deep sigh.

David's son Absalom is out their somewhere hunting his father, wanting him dead. The king ran for his life hiding in the wilderness. His loyal bodyguards followed and a few scouts were up front.

"Why am I running like this? Why is Absalom so determined to kill me?" King David ran all the questions through his mind.

He finally found a place between two large boulders to camp for the night. The stars shined brightly, and the ground was damp. After lighting a fire and cooking dinner David's thoughts went to home.

But it wasn't his family or the kingly comforts of the palace he was thinking of. The gold utensils or his feather bed were not on his mind.

What he missed most, and what captured most of his thoughts, was the visible majesty of the Divine Presence, that hovered between the cherubim above the mercy seat on the Ark of the Covenant. David longed to be able to return to Mount Zion and see the manifest presence of God again. He missed God's presence dearly.

David's separation from God's revealed presence caused big wet tears to roll down his red cheeks. They rolled over his dry lips into his mouth. He had never had such an ache in his heart as he did now—banned from Jerusalem and unable to come before God's revealed presence. His passion to visit with God was denied. David picked up his harp and in desperation and frustration he sang:

> As the deer pants for the water brooks, so pants my
> soul for You, O God. My soul thirsts for God, for
> the living God. When shall I come and appear before
> God? My tears have been my food day and night, while
> they continually say to me, "Where is your God?"
> Psalms 42:1–3 KJV

HUNGRY

Have you been that hungry for the Lord's nearness? Have you been so thirsty for Him that you cried out to God, day and night, wanting to know His presence?

David's burning desire for the Lord was intense—an extreme thirst. It was like the thirst of a deer running from pursuing dogs nearly exhausted. The singer felt like a hunted creature, burning with inexpressible thirst and desperate for the refreshment of water. David was both homesick and heartsick for God.

God's presence took David from the fields and made him Israel's greatest king. Born in 1040 BC, he was the youngest son of Jesse of Bethlehem. As the smallest son of the family, he was assigned, as soon as he was old enough, to tend the sheep. Required to spend long hours at these duties, David chose to take advantage of the time to get to know God. David loved the Lord very much.

I will love you, O Lord, my strength.
Psalms 18:1 KJV

Because David loved the Lord, he was secretly anointed king of Israel at a very young age. His passion for God gave him favor with God and was filled with the Spirit of the Lord as a young teenager (1 Samuel 16:13).

David learned to play a harp and used it as he sang spontaneous praises to God and developed a deeply personal relationship with Him. As a young boy he discovered the greatness of Jehovah-Shammah—the Lord who is present. David was not afraid to approach God for he knew God and knew His goodness. So great was David's love for the Lord that his soul ached to be with Him. He was thirsty for God's manifest presence.

THE SINGER FELT LIKE A HUNTED CREATURE, BURNING WITH INEXPRESSIBLE THIRST

David's passion for the Lord's presence did not end when he became king. He honored the Ark of the Covenant, where God's presence dwelled. When the Ark remained for a time in another land, because of an accident that had occurred in transporting it, David was not pleased. He could not rest until the Ark (on which was the presence of God) was retrieved and brought back to Jerusalem.

David consulted with the captains of thousands
and hundreds, and with every leader. And
David said to all the congregation of Israel "…
Let us bring the ark of our God back to us."
…David and all Israel went up Baalah, to
Kirjath Jearim, to bring up from there the
Ark of God the Lord, who dwells between the
cherubim, where His name is proclaimed.
1 Chronicles 13:1–3, 6 KJV

David prepared a special tent where the Ark could dwell safely so that he could have God's presence always near him.

David built houses for himself in the City
of David; and he prepared a place for the
ark of God, and pitched a tent for it.
…So it was, when God helped the Levites who bore
the ark of the covenant of the Lord, that they offered
seven bulls and seven rams.

HE COULD NOT REST UNTIL THE PRESENCE OF GOD WAS RETRIEVED

…Thus all Israel brought up the
ark of the covenant of the Lord
with shouting and with the sound
of the horn, with trumpets and
with cymbals, making music with
stringed instruments and harps.
…So they brought the ark of God, and set it in the
midst of the tabernacle that David had erected for it.
…He appointed some of the Levites to
minister before the ark of the Lord.
1 Chronicles 15:1, 26, 28; 16:1, 4 KJV

When the people of Israel caught David's vision to bring back the Ark, to bring back the manifest presence of the Lord into their lives, they did it with great celebration. They got noisy. Joyful singing and exuberant praise is still one of the most significant ways we can bring the presence of God into our lives.

Most people who believe in the presence of God also believe that this presence can be felt only when and where God chooses. However, the Bible teaches us that we can experience His presence every time we sing His praises (Psalms 100:2).

David further honored the Ark of the Covenant by permanently installing the ministry of Levitical singers under Asaph. He encouraged Asaph and his associates to write and sing psalms. His passion for the Lord's presence can be seen in the seventy-three psalms that bear his name. This king was a worshiper and constantly praised the Lord.

David personally compiled the first psalter or collection of these songs (Psalms 1–41). They are called psalms because of the root word "psalter" that means "harp songs." David often played his harp when he worshiped in God's presence, his worship songs became known as psalms.

The Psalms contain tremendous insights into the presence of the Lord. For example: We can discover how to enter His presence in Psalm 100. We can find out what type of praise God likes best in Psalm 22. We can see the effect high praise has on God's enemies in Psalm 149. And we can learn how various expressions of praise and worship are directly associated with the manifest presence of the Lord.

DAVID HAD A BURDEN TO HONOR THE LORD BY BUILDING A GLORIOUS TEMPLE FOR HIS MANIFEST PRESENCE

Later, David wanted to build a more permanent house for the Ark of the Covenant.

> When David was settled in his palace, he summoned
> Nathan the prophet. "Look," David said, "I am
> living in a beautiful cedar palace, but the Ark of
> the Lord's Covenant is out there under a tent!"
> 1 Chronicles 17:1 NLT

David had a burden to honor the Lord by building a glorious temple for His manifest presence. Although he was not permitted to build such a temple in his lifetime, he left explicit instructions for his son Solomon and his assistants.

David became widely renowned as the greatest King of Israel because his passion for the presence of the Lord.

> David became greater and greater, for
> the Lord of hosts was with him.
> 1 Chronicles 11:9 ESV

The manifest presence of God brought favor and blessings into David's life despite the foolish decisions and disappointments he experienced. Fundamentally, David's heart was always passionately pursuing the presence of God. This can be said of you as well. Do you want to know the favor and blessings of God as David did?

CHAPTER TWENTY
STUDY GUIDE

SCRIPTURE

Read Psalms 42 and 1 Chronicles 15.

QUESTIONS

1. Who was David running from?

2. What did David miss more than anything else as a fugitive from Jerusalem?

3. How did what David missed affect him?

4. What was David's normal practice when he was home and in front of the Ark?

5. How does David model for us how to connect with God's presence?

6. What were some of the ways we can connect with the presence of God that David wrote about?

REFLECTION

1. Have you missed the manifest presence of the Lord so much that it affected you emotionally?

2. What do you take away from David's example to us of someone passionate about the manifest presence of God?

3. What is the Holy Spirit saying to you through this chapter?

PRAYER / CONFESSION

Heavenly Father,

I am touched by David's passion for your manifest presence. Put within me a greater thirst for You.

I desire to make your presence a priority and a passion in my life. I desire to converse with You often and be deliberate in my pursuit of your revealed presence.

In Jesus Name,

Amen

MEDITATE / MEMORIZE

As the deer pants for the water brooks, so pants my
soul for You, O God. My soul thirsts for God, for
the living God. When shall I come and appear before
God? My tears have been my food day and night, while
they continually say to me, "Where is your God?"
Psalms 42:1–3 KJV

21

CHAPTER TWENTY-ONE
OBED-EDOM

○──○

The word was out! The Ark had returned to Israel. Worshipers came from all over the country—young and old, rich and poor. Everyone was excited about the Ark of the Covenant, and the visible glory of God, returning to Jerusalem. They were excited that the divine presence was with them.

A musical parade of pageantry and festivity quickly formed. The Ark rode majestically on a plain wooden cart pulled by two young oxen. Uzza and Ahio drove the oxen steering the cart as it slowly proceeded along the country road toward Jerusalem.

Musicians were playing stringed instruments including harp, trumpets, tambourines and cymbals. All the people sang joyously as their parade moved toward Jerusalem. It was a festive scene.

When the procession arrived at Chidon, something terrible happened that no one anticipated. The oxen pulling the cart bearing the Ark, suddenly stumbled and the Ark started sliding. Uzza put out his hand to steady the ark and was instantly struck dead by the power and anger of the Lord.

David was stunned! "Why did Uzza die?" David couldn't believe it. "What did we do wrong?" He asked God.

God didn't answer David. No answer was an answer of sorts. It caused David to research how to carry the Ark. It forced David to the books of Moses, and there it says when the Ark of the Covenant is moved it is to be placed on the shoulders of the Levites, which in David's day were the singers.

David was both angry and afraid. How could they ever get the Ark back to Jerusalem if nobody could touch it? He had to figure this out. Until then he had to do something with the Ark. David decided to leave the Ark under the care of a local farmer until he could decide what to do with it. Before he brought the Ark to Jerusalem David wanted to figure out how he should move it as well as prepare a place for it.

The Ark was taken to the home of a man named Obed-Edom. I can just imagine what happened…

Obed-Edom and his family are enjoying a quiet meal together at the end of a very busy day, when suddenly there is a loud knock at the door. Obed-Edom quickly arises and goes to the door to open it. What he sees startles him.

Before his humble threshold stands a man dressed in Levitical attire. Behind him stands a great entourage of people, looking on. Many of the men appear to be musicians. Obed-Edom doesn't notice the body hanging over one of the donkeys or the presence of the king in the midst of the singers.

"Yes? May I help you?" he asks finally.

"Are you Obed-Edom?" the man asks urgently.

"Yes, I am," he replies, all the while wondering what all this commotion could be about. Why was a group of musicians standing in front of his house? Who was this strange man? And what did they want with him?

"You see that man standing at the center of the musicians?" continues the Levite. "That is King David. He is wondering if you…"—His voice drops off as if he is having difficulty expressing what is on his mind.

"Yes?" prompts Obed-Edom, standing on his tiptoes to get a better look at the king.

THE ATMOSPHERE… IMMEDIATELY CHANGED WHEN THE ARK OF GOD CAME THROUGH THE DOOR

"Well," said the Levite. "Would you keep God for a while?

"Ah—What I mean is that King David wants to leave the Ark of the Covenant here for a while. Would you mind?"

Stunned, Obed-Edom slowly replies, "Sure. Well, maybe I had better check with my wife. Could you wait a moment?"

Obed-Edom disappears for a moment behind the door and excitedly tells his wife, "Honey, King David wants to know if we would mind keeping God for a while. It's okay, isn't it?"

Within seconds he re-emerges proudly stating, "That would be fine. Put Him right here next to the TV."

The Levites pick up the Ark by its extension and carry it into the house setting it softly down on the living room, where it will stay for the next three months.

Can you imagine? The illustrious presence of God was in Obed-Edom's home.

PROSPER

Those were glorious days for Obed-Edom's family! The atmosphere in their home immediately changed when the Ark of God came through the door. The entire household was blessed.

> The ark of God remained with the family of Obed-
> Edom in his house three months. And the Lord blessed
> the house of Obed-Edom and all that he had.
> 1 Chronicles 13:14

EVERYTHING IN THEIR LIVES PROSPERED BECAUSE OF THE MANIFEST PRESENCE

Everything in their lives prospered because of the manifest presence of God. The children were unusually obedient and courteous. They received top grades at school and really didn't have to study much. It was as if the answers just came to them.

Obed-Edom's wife's garden did very well that spring. Her onions were nearly as large as basketballs. The olive harvest was triple what it was other years, and the olives were as large as grapefruits.

The cattle, the donkeys, and the sheep all were fruitful and bore young that year. Even the family pet had a very large litter.

So many things had changed. There was such peace in the household. The family loved to just sit around the living room together in the evenings enjoying each other and the presence of God.

DEPARTED

Three months later, the family was having their evening meal when the oldest son heard a commotion outside and jumped up to look outside and see what was happening. Just then there was a knock on the door. When Obed-Edom opened the door, he found standing there the same Levite who had visited him ninety days earlier.

"Yes? May I help you?" Obed-Edom asks.

"Mr. Obed-Edom," replies the Levite, "Is God still here? We have come for Him."

"Yes, He's in the living room, where you left Him," he replied.

"We have immensely enjoyed Him living with us. Thank you for the privilege of having Him in our house."

Obed-Edom and his family stood back in hushed silence as the Levites entered the house, and picked up the holy box and carried it out through the front door by its long poles. The procession of musicians and singers faded in the distance toward Jerusalem.

Obed-Edom and his family stood at the door watching God's presence disappear over the horizon. Almost afraid to move or speak they all stood in silence, not quite realizing what had just happened.

Finally Obed-Edom said, "Let's go inside."

The door was shut, and the family sat in silence in the living room, each one staring at the space that once glowed with the presence of the Lord.

No one said a word. Everyone was downhearted and despondent. They all realized that there was now a huge hole in their lives. Something was majorly missing, and it felt wrong. It was like someone very close to the family had left and they never knew when they would see them again.

A little later, the Bible records the names of the men who were chosen to keep the doors of the house of the Lord. Among them is the name Obed-Edom.

> "...And with them their relatives of the
> second rank ... Obed-Edom and Jeiel, the
> gatekeepers... Obed-Edom, Jeiel and Azaziah,
> to lead with lyres tuned to the sheminith."
> 1 Chron 15:18–21 KJV

> He appointed some of the Levites as ministers
> before the ark of the Lord, even to celebrate and to
> thank and praise the LORD God of Israel: Asaph
> the chief, and second to him Zechariah, then Jeiel,
> Shemiramoth, Jehiel, Mattithiah, Eliab, Benaiah,
> Obed-Edom and Jeiel, with musical instruments,
> harps, lyres; also Asaph played loud-sounding cymbals,

and Benaiah and Jahaziel the priests blew trumpets
continually before the ark of the covenant of God…"
1 Chronicles 16:4–6 NASB

"…Obed-Edom, Jeiel, and Azaziah
were chosen to play the lyres."
1 Chronicles 16:5 NLT

HE TASTED THE SWEET PRESENCE OF GOD... AND IT CHANGED ...THE DESTINY OF HIS FAMILY

Apparently he had left the farm and moved to Jerusalem with all his family in order to be near the Ark—to be near God. This family had grown accustomed to God's presence. Life without God's presence no longer had any meaning for them.

Historians and Bible scholars proposed that Obed-Edom, a converted Philistine, became a Levite—a singer before the Ark. He changed his career because of his encounter with God's manifested presence in his home. He had tasted the sweet presence of God intimately, and it changed his destiny and the destiny of his family.

Do you want that? Do you want God's presence in your life, in your home and with those you love?

What are you willing to do to know God's revealed presence in your life? To what lengths would you go? What sacrifices would you make to be closer to God?

Have you experienced that same longing for God's revealed presence? Does your family want to be near God, to live in His manifest presence? You can. He calls you into His presence. You may have to leave something behind in order to meet Him, but if His presence is important to you, that won't matter. Nothing is more important than being close to God's presence.

CHAPTER TWENTY-ONE
STUDY GUIDE

SCRIPTURE

Read 1 Chronicles 13.

QUESTIONS

1. What does the Ark of the Covenant mean to King David and Israel?

2. What happened to stop the musical procession of the Ark?

3. What did David and the procession do wrong?

4. What was David's concern regarding the Ark?

5. What did David do with the Ark of the Covenant while he prepared a place for it?

6. Why did God bless the house of Obed-Edom?

7. What occurred that caused Obed-Edom to relocate his family to Jerusalem?

REFLECTION

1. How does Obed-Edom's encounter with God's manifest presence affect you?

2. What would you do differently to encounter God after reading this chapter

3. What is the Holy Spirit saying to you through this chapter?

PRAYER / CONFESSION

Heavenly Father,

I want to know your manifest presence like Obededom. Show me how to experience your presence in my home with my family.

I will do what is necessary to know your presence with my family. Give us the desire to make the sacrifices to know You more intimately.

In Jesus Name,

Amen

MEDITATE / MEMORIZE

The ark of God remained with the family of Obed-Edom in his house three months. And the Lord blessed the house of Obed-Edom and all that he had.
1 Chronicles 13:14

22

CHAPTER TWENTY-TWO
SATAN

○———————————————————————————————○

I was in the Ohio River valley teaching a worship seminar on music in the Bible. At the close of a worship seminar, a young, petite college student came forward for prayer. When I asked her what she wanted prayer for, she told me that during the worship she had a strong desire to strangle her mother, who was worshiping the Lord next to her.

It didn't take much discernment to know that this was the work of spiritual darkness. Satan always wants to traumatize and terrorize God's people.

> The thief comes only to steal and kill and destroy.
> John 10:10 NIV

It was interesting to me that the deadly compulsion did not come to the young woman before the service, or during the offering, or even during the preaching of the Word. The enemy was attacking her during the spontaneous worship, when God's presence was being manifested.

I knew I was dealing with a strong spiritual power, but I prayed for her anyway hoping there would be no manifestation. Just then she fell to the ground, her mouth expanded, and a very deep masculine voice began to speak to me. She was in a trance, and another personality took over her body. I was startled and couldn't believe what I was witnessing.

THE ANGELS CAME TO PRESENT THEMSELVES BEFORE THE LORD, AND SATAN ALSO CAME

When she came to, she joined her mother and left. I asked the pastor about her situation. He said her mother is the Women's Aglow director in their state, and she had problems with her daughter. The young woman would go into a rage and move small pieces of furniture in their home without touching them.

Many years later I was speaking at a master intensive course study for a prominent university, and I met that same pastor. I asked him about the young woman. He said she is married now, serves at her local church, and is free of the darkness that once harassed her.

I was so grateful to hear that God triumphed in that woman's life and that she was free from the presence of evil spirits. Now when she worships, she is not troubled with darkness and can enjoy the manifest presence of God.

BEFORE GOD

Satan too once had the privilege of entering into God's presence—in the heavenly realm. However, he lost that privilege.

> One day the angels came to present themselves
> before the Lord, and Satan also came with them.
> Job 1:6 NIV

We know that the manifest presence of the Lord constrains and suppresses Satan. When we praise the Lord, He manifests His nearness, and spiritual darkness is repelled. How is it possible, then, that Satan could just walk right into the presence of God and carry on a conversation with Him?

> "Where have you come from?" the Lord asked Satan.
> Satan answered the Lord, "I have been patrolling
> the earth, watching everything that's going on."
> Job 2:27 NLT

The Bible says that after Satan finished talking with God, Satan went out from the presence of the Lord (Job 1:12). The same language is used here as in Psalms 100:2 (where the Lord encourages us to come into His presence with singing). Satan was possibly in that same dimension of God's presence as we now experience. Why? How is that possible? The accuser admitted that he had been out searching for prey. And yet God admitted him into His presence.

Jesus, through His death on the cross and His resurrection from the dead, provided for us an entrance into the manifest presence of God. At the same time, He recaptured the keys of death, hell, and the grave and, thus, placed definite boundaries upon Satan's activities.

Personally, I believe that Satan no longer has access to the reveled presence of God. He can no longer just stroll into the throne room of heaven—when and if he feels like it. When Jesus died on the cross it changed everything. It marked the beginning of the end for him.

Ezekiel revealed Satan's former position:

> You were in Eden, the garden of God. You were the
> anointed Cherub who covers. I established you. You
> were on the holy mountain of God; You walked
> back and forth in the midst of fiery stones.
> Ezekiel 28:13-14 NIV

Some Bible scholars believe that this portion of scripture speaks of Satan before his fall. He was close to God. Satan had covered the throne of God and led the heavens in worship to God. "The holy mountain of God," we believe, was the place of worship and the place of sacrifice.

EVICTION

Satan walked in the midst of the stones of fire. These were the angelic luminaries who were in the fiery presence of God. But Satan rebelled against God's authority and tried to exalt himself above his Maker. Because of that, he was removed from the presence of the Lord.

THIS WICKED SPIRIT WAS EVICTED AND EXPELLED FROM GOD'S MANIFEST PRESENCE

I cast you out as a profane thing from the mountain of God, and the guardian cherub drove you out from the midst of the stones of fire. Your heart was proud and lifted up because of your beauty; you corrupted your wisdom for the sake of your splendor. I cast you to the ground.
Ezekiel 28:16-17 Amplified

Satan's greatest punishment was to be banished from the presence of Almighty God. This wicked spirit was evicted and expelled from God's manifest presence. Isaiah also spoke of his fall.

How are you fallen from heaven, O light-bringer and day-star, son of the morning! How you are cut down to the ground, you who weakened and laid prostrate the nations. O Blasphemous, Satanic king of Babylon! And you said in your heart, I will ascend to Heaven; I will exalt my throne above the stars of God; I will sit upon the mount of the assembly in the uttermost north;
Isaiah 14:12-13 Amplified

Despite his fall, Satan hasn't given up his ravenous ambition to rule in Zion. Another version states His declaration as:

I will sit also upon the mount of the congregation, in the sides of the north.
Isaiah 14:13 KJV

This was Satan's declaration of war with God, for the Almighty God sat on the sides of the north.

> Beautiful for situation, the joy of the whole earth,
> is mount Zion, on the sides of the north.
> Psalms 48:2 KJV

The church is spiritual Mount Zion:

> But you have come to Mount Zion and to the
> city of the living God, the heavenly Jerusalem,
> to an innumerable company of angels.
> Hebrews 12:22

Satan wants to be the object of our praise, to sit where God sits, in the praises of His people. That is what he meant when he said, "I will sit also upon the mount of the congregation." God is sitting there; but Satan wants to sit there as well. He wants God's place.

> But You are holy, O You Who dwell in [the Holy
> Place where] the praises of Israel [are offered].
> Psalms 22:3 Amplified

The word "dwell" here means to sit or ascend to the throne. When we praise the Lord, He comes and sits on the throne of our praise. He rules in our midst. I believe that Satan's desire is to sit in the midst of the worshiping church. He wants to sit where God sits, where God's throne is. He wants to be restored to the presence of the Lord. Since God will not restore him, he seeks to invade the manifest presence of the Lord as we worship.

Satan wants to be worshiped too. He wants to sit in God's seat. He wants to control you and rule your life. As the scripture says, submit to God and resist the Devil, and he will flee. Don't entertain darkness of any kind in music, games, or TV. Christians are to forcibly oppose the Devil.

Secondly, become a worshiper, a person of God's presence who has a genuine desire to be with Him. Passionately pursue the revealed presence of God and encounter the power of His presence.

CHAPTER TWENTY-TWO
STUDY GUIDE

SCRIPTURE

Read Ezekiel 28 and Isaiah 14.

QUESTIONS

1. In the story of the college student, when was she having thoughts of strangling her mother?

2. Describe the time when Satan came into the presence of God.

3. When God asked Satan what he had been doing, what did he say?

4. What was Satan's former position and responsibility in heaven before he was evicted?

5. The author believes it is Satan's desire to dwell in the midst of the worshiping church. Why is that?

6. How has Satan declared war with God?

7. How can we repel Satan?

REFLECTION

1. How has Satan tried to influence you?

2. What did you do to repel Satan?

3. What is the Holy Spirit saying to you through this chapter?

PRAYER / CONFESSION

Heavenly Father,

I am grateful that you invite me and allow me to come into your presence. It is my desire to know your presence more personally.

I will resist the Devil's presence and puruse your revealed nearness. Your presence is my safe place.

In Jesus Name,

Amen

MEDITATE / MEMORIZE

> But You are holy, O You Who dwell in [the Holy
> Place where] the praises of Israel [are offered].
> Psalms 22:3 Amplified

CHAPTER TWENTY-THREE

HIS PERSON

○———————————————————————————————————○

M y wife was in the bedroom getting ready for our date. She took her time because she wanted to look her best for her husband. When she came into the room, the air was filled with the most pleasant fragrance. I knew she was near because I could smell her.

I could have followed her wherever she went simply by searching for her with my nose. Her presence was revealed by the fragrance she wore. I could recognize it anywhere.

In the same sense, the presence of God is like His cologne. It catches our attention and makes us aware that He is near. But the presence is not the person. The "person of Jesus" should be the object of our adoration, not the "presence of Jesus."

If I were only satisfied with finding the trail of where my wife has been and didn't desire to find her my focus would be misdirected. What if I walked around the room sniffing and enjoying the perfume of her presence and ignored her? How tragic would that be? I would be seeking the evidence of her presence and not the person that is my wife.

It is important to distinguish between the outward manifestation of God's presence and His person. During our worship, some of us may be guilty of focusing on the evidence of His presence and not on the Lord Himself. Sensing that He is near because of what we see or hear or feel, we are tempted to dwell on the obvious and to ignore the not so obvious—Him Whom we cannot see. The purpose of the indications of God's presence is to draw us to Him. When that manifestation becomes the center of our attention, we err and grieve the heart of God.

Mortal man is inherently idolatrous. Humanity will invariably worship something, sometimes anything. As believers, we seek to center man's attention on our Creator and Savior. He must be the object of our desire. Yet it seems so easy for believers to get sidetracked and to concentrate on things that they can see and hear and touch, rather than on the person of the Divine One.

This is very dangerous. When we are guided by the senses, we can be easily manipulated and misled. Music can move us. Eloquent oratory can impress us. Even evil spirits can deceive us. When, however, our only focus is the person of our God, nothing can move us away from him or deceive us.

OBJECT

> The true worshipers will worship the Father in spirit and
> truth; for the Father is seeking such to worship Him.
> John 4:23 KJV

You see we worship the Father, not the presence of the Father. So we must keep in mind that, though we desire to encounter the presence of God, we must not worship the presence. We should look past the presence of God and see the person of God.

God—Father, Son, and Holy Spirit—is the proper object of our adoration.

I am in the Father and the Father in me.
John 14:11 KJV

Even angels are instructed to worship Jesus (Hebrews 1:6). We see this focus at Christ's birth; angels worshiped Him with antiphonal singing. In heaven, the elders and the living creatures worship Him (Revelation 4:9-11). He is the center and focus of heaven's worship.

LOOK PAST THE PRESENCE OF GOD AND SEE THE PERSON OF GOD

FOCUS

Sometimes I wonder if too much of our praise focuses on what God does for us rather than on Who He is. If our attention to God dwells on His provision for us, it can sometimes be a carnal pursuit. Some of us worship Him because of what we hope to gain from the relationship, not because of Who He is.

It is wonderful to praise God for His provisions, but it is more wonderful to praise Him because He is the Provider. It is wonderful to praise Him because He saves us, but it is better to praise Him because He is the Savior. It is wonderful to praise Him because He heals us, but it is better to praise Him because He is the Healer.

Our worship must not be based on need. It is based on our love of His person. Worship the exalted Christ, the Jesus of divine revelation.

When the Lord makes His presence known to us, our immediate response should be to worship Him, not to present our wish list. Knowing God only as the Source of all our needs does not inspire the high praises that He yearns to receive from His people.

When we get married, it is because we have fallen in love with a person, not because we need a cook. Worship of God must be very much like our most intimate expressions of love to our spouses. We don't talk about the bills that are due in our intimate moments together. That would surely cheapen the expression of our love.

Thanksgiving and praise are often responses to Christ's deeds. Worship, on the other hand, is always focused on His person. Worship or adoration is one person responding to another person—in love.

The manifestation of God's presence permits us to worship effectively because it enables us to catch a glimpse of the exalted person of Christ. The revelation of His presence lifts our worship to a higher level.

OUR WORSHIP MUST NOT BE BASED ON NEED RATHER OUR LOVE OF HIS PERSON

When John the Beloved encountered the presence of Jesus, he first heard a voice. To him, it sounded like a trumpet. It was both loud and authoritative. He heard the voice say:

> "I am the Alpha and the Omega, the First and the
> Last," and, "What you see, write in a book and
> send it to the seven churches which are in Asia."
> Then I turned to see the voice that spoke with me.
> Revelation 1:11–12 KJV

When John heard the voice of the Lord, he turned, expecting to see something. He expected to see Jesus. His focus was not on the voice but from whom the voice was coming.

> And having turned I saw seven golden lampstands,
> and in the midst of the seven lampstands One like
> the Son of Man, clothed with a garment down to
> the feet and girded about the chest with a golden
> band. His head and hair were white like wool, as
> white as snow, and His eyes like a flame of fire.
> Revelation 1:12–14 KJV

What a glorious experience! Most of us would give anything to see what John saw and to hear what John heard. But if you imagine that this experience is reserved for a chosen few, you're wrong! I want to tell you that you can have an experience similar to that of John the Revelator—if you are willing to concentrate on the person of Jesus, listen for His voice, and take time to turn to see Him.

If we are willing to seek God as John did, God is ready and willing to reveal Himself to us. Our victorious Champion stands in resplendent glory, looking longingly in your direction with those eyes "like a flame of fire."

John described Him further:

> His feet were like fine brass, as if refined in a furnace,
> and His voice as the sound of many waters:
> Revelation 1:15 KJV

His voice was like white noise. It contains all the frequencies sounding simultaneously, the combination of all the sound waves we can hear. What a voice!

> He had in His right hand seven stars, out of His
> mouth went a sharp two-edged sword, and His
> countenance was like the sun shining in its strength.
> Revelation 1:16 KJV

Can anyone look into the sun and not be affected by its brilliance? Jesus' brilliance was as the sun at its brightest. Can anyone look at the Son and not be affected by His brilliance? John said:

> When I saw Him, I fell at His feet as dead.
> Revelation 1:17 KJV

This is the appropriate response to the revelation of God's presence. Many people have heard the Lord speak to them; many others have looked to see Him. But few fall prostrate at His feet. John was not forced to fall before the Lord, but his heart would not permit him to do otherwise. The heart of a true worshiper finds only one appropriate expression, that of total prostration; for the glory of God's presence causes a mixture of gut-wrenching fear, reverence, and profound worship.

> He laid His right hand on me, saying to me, "Do not be
> afraid; I am the First and the Last. I am He who lives,
> and was dead, and behold, I am alive forever- more.
> Amen. And I have the keys of Hades and of Death."
> Revelation 1:17–18 KJV

John was seeing the victorious Champion, He Who has triumphed from the beginning of history and Who will continue to triumph till the end of time. This was His Eminence, the Eternal One. Praise God forever and ever! When John saw Him, he fainted.

OUR VICTORIOUS CHAMPION STANDS IN RESPLENDENT GLORY, LOOKING LONGINGLY IN YOUR DIRECTION

This is the revelation of the Person of our worship. He is the Center of our exaltation. He is the focus of our adoration and reverence. He is the recipient of all honor and praise. He is the One we love so dearly. Therefore we burn with a passion to be near Him. We have a passion to encounter His intimate presence made possible because of the cross.

While Jesus was on the earth, He was the presence of the Father incarnate, the very presence of God embodied, made manifest, "made flesh," the Divine mixed with the human.

> The Word [Christ] became flesh (human,
> incarnate) and tabernacled—fixed His tent of
> flesh, lived awhile—among us; and we [actually]
> saw His glory—His honor, His majesty.
> John 1:14 Amplified

Let Him become the object of your own worship.

When worship leaders in any culture stand before their respective congregations and endeavor to lead the people into God's presence, they may be challenged with these biblical words:

> Sir, we wish to see Jesus.
> John 12:21 KJV

It is not an emotion or a feeling that we personally seek and to which we seek to lead others. It is the person of the exalted Christ and the manifestation of His person. I encourage you to develop a passion for His person—a hunger and craving to know and get closer to not only the presence but the person of your love and affection.

CHAPTER TWENTY-THREE
STUDY GUIDE

SCRIPTURE

Read Revelation 1.

QUESTIONS

1. How is God's person different than His presence?

2. What is God's purpose in manifesting His presence?

3. In our worship do we often focus on His presence or His person?

4. How can we be deceived in our worship?

5. If we focus our praise on God's provision, why is that not as good as praising Who He is?

6. Praise may focus on what God has done, but what should our worship focus on and why?

7. What was John's reaction to encountering the presence of God?

REFLECTION

1. How can you focus more on God's person than His presence?

2. What would you do differently after reading this chapter?

3. What is the Holy Spirit saying to you through this chapter?

PRAYER / CONFESSION

Heavenly Father,

I desire to know you more intimately and realize to do that I must focus on getting to know who You are.

I want to know your peronality and your how You think and do things. Reveal to me who You are.

In Jesus Name,

Amen

MEDITATE / MEMORIZE

> And having turned I saw seven golden lampstands,
> and in the midst of the seven lampstands One like
> the Son of Man, clothed with a garment down to
> the feet and girded about the chest with a golden
> band. His head and hair were white like wool, as
> white as snow, and His eyes like a flame of fire.
> Revelation 1:12–14 KJV

MANIFEST

At least believe it on the evidence of these works.
John 14:11 KJV

MANIFEST PRESENCE

were ministering to
hat to do so I
while I was
behaving

God's
ise

CHAPTER TWENTY-FOUR

DARKNESS

I was leading a worship service in a resort town in Mexico with four musicians from the US. The sermon had just ended, and the minister encouraged us to lift our voices in praise to the Lord. The worship team and I led a song in Spanish, and the congregation joined us.

After we had praised together for a while, we began to sing spontaneously, and there was an unusual sense that God was very near. People began to come forward and present themselves to the Lord. Some were believers from the local church, but many others were visitors from outside the congregation. All of them were responding to an unseen presence of God that was drawing them to the front.

Christians began to encircle those who had come forward to be prayed for. After about twenty minutes, one of the ladies who had come for prayer got down on her hands and knees and began to crawl, hissing like a cat. The Christians increased their prayer fervor, while the musical team continued singing spontaneously to the Lord.

The woman tried to crawl away from those wh[o] her in prayer, continuing to hiss loudly.

As a young worship leader I didn't know exactly [w] continued leading the spontaneous praises to God. All th[e] asking myself, "What was happening here? Why is this wom[an] so oddly?"

ONE OF THE LADIES ... BEGAN TO CRAWL HISSING LIKE A CAT

I realized later that the power of presence we were encountering during the pr[aise] had disturbed the spirit world. The darkness [in] this woman, normally hidden, began to reveal itself making her act like an animal. She was under the influence of an evil spirit. It was interesting to note that this did not happen during the preaching or during the song service, but during the time of spontaneous praise and prayer.

This strange scene actually happened and is a witness to the fact that God inhabits the praises of His people. When we sing our worship to Him, we can expect to experience His presence in very real ways. When darkness begins to expose itself, it is a sign, or indication, that God is present in power to free those enslaved.

There is an increasing awareness among believers of God's revealed presence that occurs in worship. When the Lord reveals Himself in the midst of worship by His people, He provides a witness, a testimony of His glory. This witness takes three forms. First, there is a witness to the spirit world—the kingdom of darkness. Second, there is a witness to the unbeliever. And third, there is a witness to the believer.

SPIRIT WORLD

Dr. Sam Sasser, the man whom God used to help me understand the power of spontaneous singing, once told me about an experience he had as a missionary in the Marshall Islands.

When he was on the island of Yap in the Eastern Caroline Islands, he was challenged by the old village chief, who wanted to prove that his ancestral god was greater than this Christian God that Dr. Sasser preached. He confronted Dr. Sasser in a public meeting where some two thousand men were standing in a circle in a five-acre field.

"The god that we serve is ten times stronger than anything you have ever seen," the chief boldly declared.

He said, "I'll prove it," then began clapping his hands and singing in a dissonant minor mode. The other men joined him. None of them were singing the same thing. They were singing extemporaneously. Two women entered the circle and began dancing with their hands raised. Soon the women rose ten feet into the air.

"What do you think about that?" the chief asked.

Dr. Sasser admitted to me, "I was afraid and began shaking!"

"I walked into the center of the circle and began to sing a spontaneous praise to Jesus. Within twenty seconds both of the women fell to the ground."

The men who sat in the circle, obviously spirit mediums, were amazed, and the presence of God had a powerful witness in that place. It didn't take two thousand Christians, just one worshiper who knew how to invoke God's revealed presence, and darkness was defeated. God indeed inhabits the praises of His people.

The manifestation of God's presence through worship broke the hold the spirit world had on these women's bodies. When they were lifted into the air and fell, they had hurt themselves. When Dr. Sasser prayed for them they were miraculously healed.

The power of God's manifest presence has the authority to drive out darkness in any situation. You have nothing to fear.

> Finally, be strong in the Lord, relying
> on his mighty strength.
> Put on the whole armor of God so that you may be
> able to stand firm against the devil's strategies
> Ephesians 6:10–11 ISV

When the Lord inhabits the praises of His people, His presence is a deterrent to the powers of darkness. His manifest presence speaks of His power, to the work Christ did at Calvary, and to the empty tomb He left when He rose from the dead.

THE POWER OF GOD'S MANIFEST PRESENCE HAS THE AUTHORITY TO DRIVE OUT DARKNESS

Christ has "disarmed principalities and powers" (Colossians 2:15). He stripped Satan of his power and left him with a hollow kingdom of darkness. The King James Version of the Bible uses the word "spoiled."

> And having spoiled principalities and powers, he made
> a show of them openly, triumphing over them in it.
> Colossians 2:15 KJV

The word "spoil" used here means to strip. Could it be that Jesus as a Master Taxidermist has stripped the Devil of his life and power and stuffed him with straw and sewed him back up?

Jesus made a public spectacle of the Devil when He rose from the grave, triumphing over him and setting his hostages free. Satan and his demonic armies had invaded earth and enslaved its inhabitants into captivity, subjecting them to his evil reign. Christ, by his death and resurrection, subdues the invaders and recaptures their prisoners.

> When you ascended to the heights,
> you led a crowd of captives.
> Psalms 68:18 NLT

Jesus made a public example of the Devil. He showed spiritual powers and principalities who was in charge. It was a public humiliation as he paraded Satan through the heavens, celebrating his defeat. As captives of war, subjugated and incarcerated by the power of Jesus, the triumphant march gave witness to the spirit world of the power of His presence.

When we worship the Lord, His presence indicates His resurrection power is present. His presence reminds the kingdom of darkness and its chief of their lack of power against our God and His people. Our enemies are impotent in the sight of God.

That is why the spirit world gets restless when we begin to worship. Spiritual darkness goes on "red alert." All sorts of alarms go off, and those who are influenced by dark powers begin to act irrationally.

The Devil doesn't want us to worship God and encounter His manifest presence. He doesn't want God to reveal Himself among us because God's manifest nearness renders useless all the powers of darkness.

The Lord inhabits His church, and His church is charging the gates of hell (meaning its power and authority). As we go forth into battle, Jesus is with us. As Israel carried the Ark of the Covenant into battle, so we carry the presence of the Lord in our worship. With His help, we can charge the very gates of hell.

In the Epistle to the Ephesians, Ignatius of Antioch, who died in 110 A.D. wrote; "Take heed, then, often to come together to give thanks to God, and show forth His praise. For when ye come frequently together in the same place, the powers of Satan are destroyed, and his "fiery darts" urging to sin, fall back ineffectual. For your concord and harmonious faith prove his destruction, and the torment of his assistants."

The presence of God in our corporeal worship displaces the power of the enemy in our minds and in the atmosphere. Our worship torments the powers of darkness because it brings the manifestation of the presence of the Almighty.

> The manifold wisdom of God might be made known by
> the church to the principalities and powers in the heavenly
> places, according to the eternal purpose which He
> accomplished in Christ Jesus our Lord, in whom we have
> boldness and access with confidence through faith in him.
> Ephesians 3:10–12 KJV

Never underestimate the significance of the witness of God's manifest presence to the powers in the heavens. Satan doesn't underestimate it. He knows that when the Church really gets serious about worshiping God, his territory is under attack, and he is in danger of losing some of his spoils.

CHAPTER TWENTY-FOUR
STUDY GUIDE

SCRIPTURE

Read Ephesians 3 & 6.

QUESTIONS

1. When God's presence is revealed, there is sometimes a witness. What is that three-fold witness?

2. What impact does the revealed presence of God have on powers of darkness?

3. What did Dr. Sasser do to defeat the spiritual power he encountered, and why did it work?

4. How does the presence of God affect spiritual darkness?

5. How did Jesus spoil Satan's power?

REFLECTION

1. Have you faced spiritual darkness, and, if so, how did it impact you?

2. What would you do differently having read this chapter?

3. What is the Holy Spirit saying to you through this chapter?

PRAYER / CONFESSION

Heavenly Father,

I want to walk in the light of your manifest presence. It is there that I will know victory over darkness.

Teach me how to maintain an attitude of worship and adoration of You so I will not only be able to express my love for You but also have the protection and power of your manifest presence.

In Jesus Name,

Amen

MEDITATE / MEMORIZE

And having spoiled principalities and powers, he made
a show of them openly, triumphing over them in it.
Colossians 2:15 KJV

25

CHAPTER TWENTY-FIVE
UNBELIEVER

○──○

An American missionary in Japan tells how the presence of God in Christian worship affected a couple that did not know the Lord:

"The congregational singing was particularly enthusiastic that morning at Living Way Church in the city of Shizuoka, southeast of Tokyo, and God's presence was nearly tangible. After the service, the two visitors approached one of the leaders with a sense of wonder. They said, 'When you were singing those songs we felt a "presence." Was that God?'[1]

The leader explained to them that they were experiencing a fulfillment of that Old Testament promise that God inhabits the praises of His people. He went on to tell them about Jesus Christ, and his words really impacted the couple. Witnessing God's presence earlier had prepared them for what he said. God's presence impacts unbelievers. This is one of the purposes of the corporeal gathering of worshipers.

─────────────

1. Gerritt Gustafson, "Worship Evangelism," Charisma Magazine, October, 1991,

When the Church gathers to worship, it gathers to witness. That is one of the reasons we worship publicly—to witness to the unbeliever of the power of our God.

Jesus said that the Son of Man came into the world "to seek and to save that which is lost" (Luke 19:10). He also came to seek true worshipers.

THERE IS A RELATIONSHIP BETWEEN OUR OUTREACH AND OUR UP-REACH

For the Father is seeking such to worship Him.
John 4:23 KJV

Our heavenly Father sent Christ to seek us and save us for the specific purpose of providing a worshiping people. The presence of God in our worship will witness to those unbelievers who are present that the Father is drawing them in with His Spirit.

POWER WITNESS

There is a relationship between the presence of God in our outreach in evangelism and our "up-reach" in worship. Worship is the goal of our evangelism, and evangelism is the natural fruit of our worship.

Unbelievers receive a witness of the presence of God when we worship. They may choose to give their lives to Christ and become disciples as worshipers themselves. As they worship, others will receive the witness of Christ, and the cycle continues.

True evangelism produces worshipers. And true worshipers want to bring others into God's presence, so they evangelize. The two are not mutually exclusive, but mutually inclusive.

Most evangelism is motivated by guilt and obligation, and those who give their lives to Christ are often introduced to an incomplete theology, void of an understanding of worship. True evangelism is born of a loving and worshiping heart. Worshipers burn with a passion to see others encounter God's manifest presence.

Without a sense of world mission and the passion that the Father about "seeking" others to be worshipers, our worship can become self-serving, as we look for only our own fulfillment that comes from being in His presence.

Worship has an evangelistic effect for the same reason that demons are confronted when we praise God, because God manifests His presence through worship. And that makes all the difference in the world!

> He who sacrifices thank offerings honors
> me, and he prepares the way so that I may
> show him the salvation of God.
> Psalms 50:23 NIV

God's manifest presence brings the conviction of sin that always precedes conversion. Wherever the living presence of Jesus is manifested, one of two things happens. Either men and women fall down and confess their sins, or they run away and hide from the presence of God.

David Wilkerson, who pastored a church in Times Square, reportedly said, "During one Tuesday night service at Times Square Church, I was overwhelmed as the presence of Jesus became manifest through the godly worshipers waiting upon Him. People came to the altar, some weeping. The fear of the Lord was awesome. I felt like Isaiah who said, 'Woe is me! for I ... am a man of unclean lips and I dwell in the midst of a people of unclean lips' (Isaiah 6:5)."

The presence of Jesus has power to destroy and drive out sin. The Psalmist declared:

> Let God arise, Let his enemies be scattered: Let those
> also that hate him flee before him. As smoke is driven
> away, so drive them away: As wax melts before the
> fire, So let the wicked perish at the presence of God.
> Psalms 68:1-2 KJV

Wickedness cannot stand in the presence of Almighty God. It must wither in His glory. The demonic strongholds that Satan has in many people's lives are dissipated when those people come into the presence of the Lord. The manifestation of God's glory frees them to make a decision to permanently come out from under the influence of darkness and live in the glorious glow of God's goodness.

Not every unbeliever responds:

"Then you will say, 'We ate and drank with
you, and you taught in our streets.'
"But he will reply, 'I don't know you or where you
come from. Away from me, all you evildoers!'"
Luke 13:26–27 NIV

THE POWER OF JESUS HAS THE POWER TO DESTROY AND DRIVE OUT SIN

Some sinners seem to take delight in the fact that they can sit in the presence of the Lord and yet remained unchanged. They resolve to remain firm and to be unaffected by God's glory. They sit among the saints whose faces glow with the glory of His presence, yet they are not moved to give their lives to Jesus. God cannot violate the free will He endowed every man with. It sounds strange but He is powerless to change the minds of those who are determined to remain closed to His will and way.

On September 15th, 1990 at a March For Jesus, more than two hundred thousand Christians filled the streets of cities all across Great Britain. They marched in unison, shouting slogans, carrying placards and singing with enthusiasm. On that day, believers in Great Britain took their worship into the streets and left a lasting witness to unbelievers.

In March of 1991, in Austin, Texas, one hundred fifty thousand Christians from one hundred twenty churches marched through the streets of the capital, invoking the presence of Jesus in prayer and praise. Similar public displays of worship have been seen in Australia, South Africa, Germany, Holland, Japan, Canada, Singapore, and other countries.

More recently two million Christians gathered in Sao Paulo, Brazil to March for Jesus.

Graham Kendrick, one of the organizers of these marches, said, "It is based on a very simple principle of taking the Church to the streets, giving glory to God, praying for His kingdom to come and His will to be done."

Graham finds the motivation for such activities in sacred Scripture:

> Oh, give thanks to the Lord! Call upon His name; Make
> known His deeds among the peoples! Sing to Him,
> sing psalms to Him; Talk of all His wondrous works.
> Psalms 105:1–2 KJV

POWER ENCOUNTER

On the Day of Pentecost, when the Holy Spirit fell on one hundred and twenty followers of Christ, those newly filled believers spilled out into the street and began openly praising God. The people of the community heard the commotion and gathered to ask: "What is this" (Acts 2:12)? After Peter explained what was happening, three thousand people gave their lives to Christ.

Worship results in the presence of Jesus revealed. When worship is public, the witness of His presence is for everyone to behold.

People are no longer asking, as in Acts, "What is this?" One reason is that so much of what the church does occurs behind closed doors. We are very protective of our privacy in worship. As a result, our worship presents very little witness to the unbeliever. Sinners are forced to enter a building where Christians regularly worship in order to experience the presence of the Lord. Could the once powerful and visible Church now be nearly invisible, as a result?

In recent years, the Holy Spirit is calling the Church back to public worship, calling us back to praise God "among the heathen."

The Scriptures challenge us:

> You are a chosen generation, a royal priesthood,
> a holy nation, His own special people, that you

may proclaim the praises of Him who called you
out of darkness into His marvelous light;
1 Peter 2:9 KJV

The Christians of the early centuries of the Church experienced the witness of God's presence in their public worship. Polycarp wrote of Christ's manifest presence that resulted in bringing Romans to repentance in the arenas of Rome.

WORSHIP RESULTS IN THE PRESENCE OF JESUS REVEALED

He reportedly said that the hearts of the believers were broken by the loss of the Christians being led into the arenas to be fed to the dogs and lions. When the bars were released and the condemned believers were forced into the arena in front of the screaming crowd, they sang praises to God. Unashamedly and with a loud voice, they sang spontaneous praise as they marched to their death.

Because of this public display of worship and faith, Polycarp reported, hundreds of Roman spectators cried out in repentance to God. The power of God's presence in the martyrs' praise changed the atmosphere for some of the spectators of this blood sport.

It was this convincing presence of Jesus that made the Church grow mightily in the first century. Nearly two millennia later, the revealed presence of the Lord Jesus Christ is still the key element of a convincing demonstration to the lost.

Oh, how we need the power of the manifest presence of Jesus to convince the world of sin and to cause the Church to grow mightily. It is the power of His presence that witnesses to the unbeliever.

CHAPTER TWENTY-FIVE
STUDY GUIDE

SCRIPTURE

Read Acts 2.

QUESTIONS

1. Jesus came into the world to seek the lost but what is God looking for as well?

2. How do the outreach of evangelism and the "up-reach" of worship go together?

3. Why does a worshiper burn with a passion to see others encounter God's manifest presence?

4. How is God's revealed presence a witness to unbelievers?

5. Why is there little witness to the unbeliever if they do not go into a worship service?

6. How does an encounter with the power of God's revealed presence impact unbelievers?

REFLECTION

1. Have you experienced a time when unbelievers were impacted by an encounter with the manifest presence of God?

2. What would you do differently after reading this chapter?

3. What is the Holy Spirit saying to you through this chapter?

PRAYER / CONFESSION

Heavenly Father,

I want to be a worshiper who encounters your manifest presence which will witness of your nearness and power to those that do not know You.

Give me a greater desire to see the unbeliever impacted by your revealed presence. Teach me how and when to worship You among those that do not know You.

In Jesus Name,

Amen

MEDITATE / MEMORIZE

You are a chosen generation, a royal priesthood,
a holy nation, His own special people, that you
may proclaim the praises of Him who called you
out of darkness into His marvelous light;
1 Peter 2:9 KJV

26

CHAPTER TWENTY-SIX
BELIEVER

Little Ana enjoyed playing with her brother André. They would often run downstairs chasing each other through the house, laughing and giggling.

One day they were playing in the hallway while their father was in prayer in his home study. In a moment of excitement, Ana and André ran down the hall and darted into their father's office. When they passed through the doorway the presence of the Lord was so strong that both of them immediately fell on the floor unconscious. The power of God's manifest presence in the room threw them to the ground.

They lay on the floor for a while as God did something in their little hearts. He was working something special in their spirits, something that would change little Ana. She recalls, "I'm not sure how long I laid on that holy ground having visions of heaven and of the Lord's angels, but I will never forget that experience." From that moment on Ana Paula Valadão had a passion to know and encounter the manifest presence of God.

That brief, yet powerful, encounter with God marked her spirit and was a definable moment in her life and ministry. It is one of the reasons she is in ministry today and has given her life to lead people before the presence and throne of God.

IMPRINT

Just like Enoch, Moses, Abraham, Jacob, Daniel, Ezekiel, Paul, John, Mary, and so many more men and woman of faith in the Bible, the power of the witness God's presence left an indelible mark in their hearts and minds.

I LAID ON THAT HOLY GROUND HAVING VISIONS OF HEAVEN AND THE LORD'S ANGELS

Men and women of old have encountered the power of God's revealed presence and been left limping, crying, shaking, and broken—marked by the very real encounter with God. Christians all over the world, just like Ana, have had their lives and hearts imprinted by an encounter with God's manifest presence.

TOUCHED

There are several ways that the manifestation of the Lord's presence witnesses to Christians. One is that it leaves an impression and desire for more of Him. Another is that it gives a sense of endearment.

When God's presence becomes very personal and poignant for a believer there is a sense of endearment or affirmation. This may happen during a worship service or during a time of waiting on God privately. Worship music is playing in the background and your heart is tender and sensitive. In those moments God may reveal or speak something very personal and powerful to you. You know it is Him because it has to do with something that only you and He know about.

Believers also feel this personal touch of God's presence during their participation in the "Eucharist," or Holy Communion, observed regularly by large numbers of believers all over the world.

> Because there is one loaf, we who are many are
> one body; for we all partake of the one loaf.
> 1 Corinthians 10:17 BSB

When we meet at the table of the Lord, God may reveal Himself to numerous believers in a very personal way. There is also a special sense of unity among brothers, a sense of true equality, a sense of God's love to each of us. It is a joyous occasion with a sense of connection with God and His family.

TRANSFORMATION

In the mystery of God's presence, we sense His love for each of us. We see His beauty manifested, and we are emotionally drawn to Him. In that moment we receive a revelation, an awareness of Who the Lord is. We become more conscious of His nature. And it changes us.

> We all, with unveiled face, beholding as in a mirror the
> glory of the Lord, are being transformed into the same
> image from glory to glory, just as by the Spirit of the Lord.
> 2 Corinthians 3:18 KJV

When we, as believers, behold the manifest presence of the Lord, we change. We become more like Jesus. This is why many believers today wish to linger in God's revealed presence.

The wonderful thing is the longer we remain in His presence, the further along we move in this process of changing into His likeness. The manifestation of His presence with us is a witness of His love for us and His desire for us to become like Him.

CONVICTION

His presence also convicts believers of sin. In the manifest presence of Him Who is sinless, we become conscious of wrong attitudes and wrong behavior. The closer we get to His presence, the more we see the imperfections in our lives and are able to deal with them.

The Scriptures admonish us:

> Repent therefore and be converted, that your sins
> may be blotted out, so that times of refreshing
> may come from the presence of the Lord.
> Acts 3:19 KJV

WHEN WE BEHOLD THE MANIFEST PRESENCE OF THE LORD WE CHANGE

The witness of Christ's revealed presence is convincing and convicting. It will not leave us unchanged but ever draws us closer to His perfect image.

HOLY SPIRIT

It is important to know that a revelation or demonstration of the Holy Spirit is similar to a manifestation of the presence of God.

In the Old Testament, the Holy Spirit empowered individuals for specific tasks. The Spirit settled upon leaders needing help in administration as in Numbers 11:16–17. Timid warriors facing formidable tasks were encouraged by the Spirit of the Lord.

> But the Spirit of the Lord clothed Gideon,
> and he sounded the trumpet, and the
> Abiezrites were called out to follow him.
> Judges 6:34 KJV

The presence or manifestation of the Holy Spirit covered Gideon and gave him the sense that God was with him. Because of the presence of the Spirit of God, Gideon arose to the occasion and stepped forward in faith.

Also, David as a teen boy experienced the manifest presence of God in the form of the Holy Spirit.

> So as David stood there among his brothers, Samuel
> took the flask of olive oil he had brought and anointed
> David with the oil. And the Spirit of the Lord came
> powerfully upon David from that day on…
> 1 Samuel 16:13 NLT

These are examples of the person of the Holy Spirit revealing Himself in a touchable and tangible way, very similarly to a manifestation of God. The Holy Spirit is part of the Trinity and has a unique function from that of Jesus the Son and God the Father. Yet all three are one. So when the Holy Spirit is moves on people or someone is filled with the Holy Spirit, it is a manifestation of God's presence.

CHAPTER TWENTY-SIX
STUDY GUIDE

SCRIPTURE

Read Acts 4.

QUESTIONS

1. In Acts 4 how were believers impacted by the manifestation of God's presence?

2. How is the manifestation of the Holy Spirit similar to the manifest presence of God?

3. How was the presence of God a witness to Jacob, Moses, or John?

4. In what way does God's presence witness to a believer today?

5. How are believers touched by the presence of God?

6. How does the presence of God transform us to be more like Jesus?

7. What impact or effect does God's revealed presence have on believers in regard to their sin?

REFLECTION

1. How has the manifest presence of God left an impression with you?

2. What would you do differently having read this chapter?

3. What is the Holy Spirit saying to you through this chapter?

PRAYER / CONFESSION

Heavenly Father,

I desire to be covered inside and out with your Holy Spirit. I want to know your revealed nearness more intimately and more powerfully.

As I linger in your presence transform me to be more like You I pray.

In Jesus Name,

Amen

MEDITATE / MEMORIZE

We all, with unveiled face, beholding as in a mirror the glory of the Lord, are being transformed into the same image from glory to glory, just as by the Spirit of the Lord.
2 Corinthians 3:18 KJV

PURSUIT

Worship is the privilege of those that seek God
with clean hands and a pure heart.

—Myles Munroe

I want the presence of God Himself, or I don't want
anything at all to do with Christianity

– A.W. Tozer

CHAPTER TWENTY-SEVEN
PRIVILEGE

○──○

God can sovereignly manifest His nearness to any person at any time; the choice and timing are His. Those unique, powerful and once-in-a-lifetime encounters with God's presence are God's choice. Like the encounter Peter had with God's presence when on the mountain with Jesus.

> He was still speaking when, behold, a bright cloud
> overshadowed them, and a voice from the cloud
> said, "This is my beloved Son, with whom I am well
> pleased; listen to him." When the disciples heard
> this, they fell on their faces and were terrified.
> Matthew 17:5–6 ESV

However, for those of us who are washed in the blood of Jesus and have made Him Lord of our lives, He has given us a special privilege—to come into the Father's presence anytime we choose.

Because of the special relationship we have with God through Jesus, we reap the special benefits of being part of the family of God. This is a greater honor than singing for the President of the United States in the White House or for the Queen of England in Buckingham Palace. Our privilege is to appear before the King of all kings, the Lord of all lords, and the President of all presidents.

A PARTICULAR PROTOCOL WAS ADVISED... FOR APPROACHING GOD

God loves for us to do it as well. He delights in being near His children.

> The person who has My commands and keeps them is the one who (really) loves Me, and whoever [really] loves Me will be loved by My Father. And I [too] will love him and will show (reveal, manifest) Myself to him — I will let Myself be dearly seen by him and make My self real to him.
> John 14:21 AMP

As we have seen throughout scripture, the desire of the Father is to be with His children. The whole purpose of the Law of Moses was to encourage the people of Israel to approach God.

> And on the eighth day he will take to him two turtledoves, or two young pigeons, and come before the Lord, to the door of the tabernacle of meeting, and give them to the priest.
> Leviticus 15:14

God's desire, when He spoke through the prophets, was that His people approach Him.

> With what shall I come before the Lord, and bow myself before God on high? Shall I come before him with burnt offerings, with calves a year old?
> Micah 6:6 ESV

Although a particular protocol was advised as necessary for approaching God, the emphasis was often on the need to approach Him, to come near to Him. This is our privilege as His children.

PREREQUISITE

The qualification or prerequisite for access into the presence of God is that you know Jesus Christ as your personal Savior and have been washed by the blood of the Lamb. It is through His blood that we can enter the Holy of Holies. It is because of what Christ did on Calvary and in the tomb that we can approach our Heavenly Father.

> For through Him we both have access
> by one Spirit unto the Father.
> Ephesians 2:18 KJV

Without a personal relationship with Jesus Christ, it is impossible to draw near to God with the full assurance of His acceptance. Although He is ever ready to receive those who want to make Him their Lord and Savior and to give their lives to Him, He said:

> I am the way, the truth, and the life. No one
> comes to the father except through Me.
> John 14:6 KJV

In order to have access to the manifest presence of Father God, it is necessary to have a personal relationship and regular fellowship with Jesus as Lord.

> The Lord is far from the wicked, but he
> hears the prayer of the righteous.
> Proverbs 15:29 KJV

Because God is everywhere, it seems odd to say that He is far from the wicked. But in the dimension of His presence that can be felt and appreciated by men, He withdraws Himself from those who refuse His ways.

The difference between "wicked" and "righteous" is the application of the blood of Jesus to our hearts and lives. We are all wicked, unless and until we have been washed in the blood of the Lamb and received forgiveness for our sins. When this takes place, we are no longer outcasts from the presence of God, and He will draw near to us.

ACCESS

Just as we have no access to salvation apart from Jesus Christ, and we have no access to heaven apart from Jesus, we have no access to His presence apart from a personal relationship with God's Son.

He is "the Way." He is "the Truth." And He is "the Life." When He said, "No one comes to the Father except through Me," He meant "no one"—no matter to which religion he or she belongs or what merit he or she might have. There are no exceptions. Christ alone is "the Way" to the Father. There is no other portal or entrance.

WALK RIGHT INTO THE FATHER'S PRESENCE, LOOK HIM IN THE FACE

> Without the shedding of blood there is no forgiveness.
> Hebrews 9:22 NIV

> This hope we have as an anchor of the soul, both sure and steadfast, and which enters the Presence behind the veil, where the forerunner has entered for us, even Jesus...
> Hebrews 6:19–20 KJV

> For Christ has not entered into the holy places made with hands ... but into heaven itself, now to appear in the presence of God for us.
> Hebrews 9:24 KJV

Because of Jesus' sacrifice on Calvary, we have the privilege of access beyond the veil of separation that once kept man from the manifest presence of the Father.

> Therefore, brethren, having boldness to enter the Holiest by the blood of Jesus, by a new and living way which He consecrated for us, through the veil, that is His flesh, and having a High Priest over the house of God, let us draw near, with a true heart in full assurance of faith.
> Hebrews 10:19–22 KJV

We can draw near to God "in full assurance." Our personal relationship with the Father gives us that assurance. His love for us and His promise to be with us guarantees it. Every single one of us can have confidence because we know that Christ is with us. We have been "accepted in the Beloved."

There is nothing more that we need to do to earn acceptance or favor with God. Jesus did it all. There is nothing more to be done to qualify us to come into His presence. Jesus finished it, making it possible for us to walk right into Father's presence, look Him in the face, and commune with Him.

FEELINGS

During a praise and worship service, when God begins to reveal His presence, some Christians began to feel very unworthy, and they become concerned. But I want to assure you that there is nothing to worry about. Feeling unworthiness in the presence of Immaculate Perfection is normal. The prophets had the same feeling. Because we are imperfect humans, it is difficult to feel totally worthy when God reveals Himself to us.

This is not cause for alarm. We know that despite our imperfections the Lord accepts us. Despite our imperfections Jesus loves us. Our loving heavenly Father, who gave us life, is ever present to comfort us in our frailties and to help us overcome every weakness.

He manifests His beloved presence not to condemn or punish us but to bless us and empower us.

CHAPTER TWENTY-SEVEN
STUDY GUIDE

SCRIPTURE

Read Hebrews 10.

QUESTIONS

1. Apart from those sovereign encounters God initiates, how is it possible to encounter God's presence anytime or place?

2. How is it a privilege to encounter God's presence?

3. What is the prerequisite for encountering God?

4. How do we have access to the manifest presence of God?

5. What is the only thing that qualifies us to enter God's presence?

6. What should we do if we feel unworthy in God's presence?

REFLECTION

1. How have you encountered God's manifest presence?

2. What would you do differently after reading this chapter?

3. What is the Holy Spirit saying to you through this chapter?

PRAYER / CONFESSION

Heavenly Father,

Thank you for the honor and privilege to come into your manifest presence. It is by the precious death and resurrection of your son Jesus that I have access.

I desire to always cherish the opportunity to enter your presence and thereby know You better. Holy Spirit help me treasure that privilege.

In Jesus Name,

Amen

MEDITATE / MEMORIZE

Therefore, brethren, having boldness to enter the Holiest
by the blood of Jesus, by a new and living way which He
consecrated for us, through the veil, that is His flesh,
and having a High Priest over the house of God, let us
draw near, with a true heart in full assurance of faith.
Hebrews 10:19–22 KJV

28

CHAPTER TWENTY EIGHT
PORTALS

○───○

Throughout history, certain men and women have been able to encounter God. Those men and women have basked in the sunshine of God's love and encountered Him in sometimes powerful and sometimes intimate ways.

SECRETS

One of the takeaways of this book is to let you know you can experience the manifest presence of God at any time or any place. You don't have to wait until Sunday when the musicians are playing and everyone is singing their praise or prayers. You can enter into His presence at any moment of any day of the year—if you are willing to learn a few simple secrets.

These strategic biblical principles, if properly applied, can lead us into the manifest presence of God. They are secrets that God has given in His

Word. Like a map, they reveal the path that leads to the rich treasure of encountering God.

Like some entrances, the gates of heaven can be hidden—not easily found. Only those who know where the doorway is can enter and enjoy heaven's delights. For example, some people keep waiting for renewal to come, while others are experiencing renewal all the time. Some people leave God's presence when they leave camp or retreat. They haven't learned to take the presence of God home with them and live in it day by day.

HE IS READY TO MANIFEST HIS PRESENCE EVERYWHERE AND ALWAYS

Other people can't feel God outside of the church building. They haven't learned that He is ready to manifest His presence everywhere and always. We don't have to lose the sense of His presence when the music stops and the musicians pack up their instruments and go home.

Just as in nature, there is a cause and effect to encountering the presence of God. There are prerequisites to entering His glory and there are ways to experience His presence. These are the principles to encountering God.

PASSAGES

There are two basic passageways into God's manifest presence: one is prayer and the other is praise. They are the twin portals that give us access to Him. When we engage in prayer or praise we are making an approach toward God.

Over and over again in scripture, believers have encountered God through prayer and praise. However these are not just any kind of prayer or praise. There is a secret to these passages that people often miss, and as a result, they don't get as close to God as they want to.

PRAYER

David said:

Let my prayer be set forth before thee as incense; and
the lifting up of my hands as the evening sacrifice.
Psalms 141:2 KJV

Our prayers are like incense from the altar, rising up before the Lord, invoking His presence.

And when he had taken the book, the four beasts
and four and twenty elders fell down before the
Lamb, having every one of them harps, and golden
vials full of odors, which are the prayers of saints.
Revelation 5:8 KJV

The golden vials that John saw contain the "odors" of prayer. There is an aroma to prayer. Prayer has a smell to it. Those who pray smell like prayer. There is a heavenly fragrance about them.

And another angel came and stood at the altar,
having a golden censer; and there was given unto
him much incense, that he should offer it with the
prayers of all saints upon the golden altar which
was before the throne. And the smoke of the
incense, which came with the prayers of the saints,
ascended up before God out of the angel's hand.
Revelation 8:3–4 KJV

Prayer is an offering given before the throne of the Lord. It may be either spoken or sung. In either case, it ascends before God as incense.

Although God is everywhere, prayer brings us into His revealed presence. Prayer is associated with God's manifest presence and brings us into a new dimension with God.

The Lord is far from the wicked: but he
hears the prayer of the righteous.
Proverbs 15:29 KJV

God hears everything. He knows everything. He is everywhere. But He hears the prayer of the righteous in a special sense. He is near; He is present when the righteous offer prayers to Him.

> For the eyes of the Lord are over the righteous,
> and his ears are open unto their prayers: but the
> face of the Lord is against them that do evil.
> 1 Peter 3:12 KJV

YOU CAN ENTER THE PRESENCE OF THE DIVINE ANY TIME AND ANY PLACE

The face of the Lord, synonymous with the presence of the Lord, is "against them that do evil." His eyes are "over the righteous." He is present to see and hear us when we pray.

> Now therefore, O our God, listen to the prayer of
> your servant and to his pleas for mercy, and for
> your own sake, O Lord, make your face [presence]
> to shine upon your sanctuary, which is desolate.
> Daniel 9:17 ESV (brackets added)

Daniel understood that prayer invokes the presence of the Lord. Daniel also experienced the presence of an angel when he prayed.

> While I was speaking in prayer, even the man
> Gabriel, whom I had seen in the vision at the
> beginning, being caused to fly swiftly, touched
> me about the time of the evening oblation.
> Daniel 9:21 KJV

You can enter the presence of the Divine at any time, in any place, through your sincere prayers to God the Father.

PRAISE

The second of the twin portals into God's presence is praise. The scriptures tell us to…

> Enter into His gates with thanksgiving
> and His courts with praise.
> Psalms 100:4 KJV

The Hebrew word for "thanksgiving" here is "towdah." It means to lift your hands, as if casting out, as a choir and offer thanks. The Hebrew word for the word "praise" in this passage is "tehillah." It means to sing spontaneous praise or to sing a new song.

> He hath put a new song in my mouth, even
> praise [tehillah] unto our God: many shall see
> it, and fear, and shall trust in the Lord.
> Psalms 40:3 KJV (brackets added)

It is not an accident that wherever worshippers sing a new song to the Lord His presence is experienced in unusual ways. This is the praise in which God has declared He dwells. God chooses to reveal Himself in tehillah.

> But you are holy, O you that inhabit
> the praises [tehillah] of Israel.
> Psalms 22:3 AKJV (brackets added)

When you have learned this wonderful secret of praise, you can come into the presence of the Lord anytime and anywhere you want to. All you have to do is sing praises and prayers to Him.

SINGING

The Bible says it again only in a different and more direct way.

> Come before His presence with singing.
> Psalms 100:2 KJV

Of all the ways that God could have chosen for us to approach Him, He chose singing. He could have chosen confession, or meditation, or silence, or even shouting. But God desires His children to come close to Him by singing to Him.

Some people, because they think they can't sing very well, feel that they are excluded from even trying to enter God's presence in this way. Surely the Lord would not like the sound of their praise, they reason. They are wrong.

If my two sons were to come to me when they were young and say, "Dad, we have a song for you," I would not reject them. Children sing in their own way. Often they don't sing the proper notes or sing off-key. Their vocal quality is poor. But as their father I would love it anyway no matter how good the singing was.

WHEREVER WORSHIPPERS SING A NEW SONG TO THE LORD HIS PRESENCE IS EXPERIENCED IN UNUSUAL WAYS

Could we imagine a father who would respond: "That's terrible, boys. Don't try to sing to me again until you can sing better!" I can't imagine it. Instead, I would want to get close to them and affectionately squeeze their cute faces and say, "I love you too!" And that is exactly the response our Heavenly Father has when you sing to Him. He loves it and opens the arms of His presence and welcomes you close because He hears your heart not your vocal ability.

God told Samuel…

> For the Lord sees not as man sees: man looks on the
> outward appearance, but the Lord looks on the heart.
> 1 Samuel 16:7 ESV

It could be said that God does not listen as man listens. Man listens to the outward—tone, pitch and quality of voice. But the Lord listens to the heart—attitude, spirit and authenticity.

Your voice may be flat, but if your heart is sincere it is the purest praise.

WINGS

These two secret portals, prayer and praise, are very closely related. In fact in the Hebrew they are almost the same word.

> Even them will I bring to my holy mountain,
> and make them joyful in my house of prayer:
> their burnt offerings and their sacrifices shall be
> accepted upon mine altar; for mine house shall
> be called an house of prayer for all people.
> Isaiah 56:7 KJV

The Hebrew word for prayer here is "tephillah." This is very close to the word for praise, "tehillah." "Tephillah" means intercession, supplication, a hymn or sacred song. Both words are musical. Prayer and praise can be sung. The two words are like the two wings of the same bird. They go together. They are the two things that cause us to mount upward into God's presence.

These two wings singing prayer and singing praise are the only two ways that I am aware of to ascend into the presence of the Lord.

PERPETUAL

Prayer and praise are to be done continually. These two are to be done perpetually because God wants us to always come close to Him.

> Pray continually.
> 1 Thessalonians 5:17 NIV

> Through Jesus, therefore, let us continually
> offer to God a sacrifice of praise — the fruit
> of our lips that confess his name.
> Hebrews 13:15 NIV

Prayer and praise are meant to be very strategic parts of every Christian's life. Are they an important part of yours? Do you pray continually? Do you continually offer to God a sacrifice of praise?

When we walk with the Lord in a continuum of prayer and praise, we will know the power of God's manifest presence in our lives in a very real way. Try it, and you will be delighted with the results. Don't be surprised when people begin to weep while you are standing in line at the grocery store—because they sense the convicting and yet comforting presence of the Lord in your life.

We were not created to live outside of God's manifest presence. Man was made for God's revealed presence. We are happiest and most satisfied in the revealed presence of God.

You make known to me the path of life; in
your presence there is fullness of joy; at your
right hand are pleasures forevermore.
Psalms 16:11 ESV

Anyone knows if you want the product to work correctly you have to follow the manufacturer's manual of operation. So it is with humanity. We do not work well, or function our best, when we are outside of God's presence.

We are like fish out of water trying to exist in an environment we were not made to live in. Life is hard, barren, bleak, tumultuous without not just Jesus but the sweetness of Jesus' manifest presence.

One day, as a Christian worship team was playing and singing in a public park, they noticed that a man, who appeared to have a tough life, began to kneel and cry out to God to help him overcome his sins. The man had sensed the presence of God as the musicians sang to God. That man got a glimpse of what all our souls cry out for: God's nearness.

I invite you to try the two portals and enter into God's presence. Begin to sing prayer and praise and see what God will do. Don't give up if it sounds strange at first. Keep singing until you sense God is near. If you don't consider yourself a singer remember--To Jesus your tone deaf singing of praise is infinitely more beautiful than your silence.

CHAPTER TWENTY-EIGHT
STUDY GUIDE

SCRIPTURE

Read Psalms 98 and Psalms 100.

QUESTIONS

1. What is one of the takeaways of this book?

2. What are the two main portals into God's revealed presence?

3. What is the Hebrew name for each portal?

4. How can we approach God through prayer?

5. How is prayer a portal to God's presence?

6. What is so special to God about us singing?

7. Why are we as humans like fish out of water?

8. Where is man the happiest and most satisfied

REFLECTION

1. How does it affect you to know that you can enter God's presence anytime and anywhere?

2. What would you do differently after reading this chapter?

3. What is the Holy Spirit saying to you through this chapter?

PRAYER / CONFESSION

Heavenly Father,

Thank You for providing the entrance into your manifest presence. I now know how to come into your presence.

I commit to use the doorways of prayer and praise to come close to You. Though I am not musical, Holy Spirit help me sing my prayers and praise for I understand the Father enjoys it. When I sing I know He will reveal Himself.

In Jesus Name,

Amen

MEDITATE / MEMORIZE

You make known to me the path of life; in
your presence there is fullness of joy; at your
right hand are pleasures forevermore.
Psalms 16:11 ESV

29

SEEK

The call is out. You have received the invitation. The Holy Spirit is drawing you into His presence. Will you seek Him? Will you sing your prayers and praise to Him?

God will not, however, force His intentions upon you. He is perfectly patient wooing you and calling you. The final decision is always and completely your own. He anxiously waits for men and women to seek Him.

> God looks down from heaven on all mankind to see if
> there are any who understand, any who seek God.
> Psalms 53:2 NIV

THE NEED

We are admonished by Scripture to put forth whatever effort is necessary to seek an intimate relationship with our Heavenly Father.

> But if from there you seek the Lord your
> God, you will find him if you seek him with
> all your heart and with all your soul.
> Deuteronomy 4:29 NIV

> Now set your mind and heart to
> seek the Lord your God...
> 1 Chronicles 22:19

These are only a few examples of the scriptures in the Bible that encourage us to search for an encounter with God. The need to seek God is one of the major themes of the Bible. The desire of the heart of God is that we actively pursue Him until we find Him. To our God, no biblical principle is more important. He wants an intimate relationship with you.

At various junctures in history, Israel's leaders recognized God's plan for them to seek Him and actively pursued Him. They encouraged others to seek Him too.

> Then they [the people of Israel] entered into a
> covenant to seek the Lord God of their fathers
> with all their heart and with all their soul.
> 2 Chronicles 15:12 KJV

> And the children of Israel, which were come again out
> of captivity, and all such as had separated themselves
> unto them from the filthiness of the heathens of
> the land, to seek the Lord God of Israel, did eat.
> Ezra 6:21 KJV

EFFORT

When you are serious about seeking the Lord, the time and effort it requires are not a deterrent to you. You will seek Him as long as it takes.

You put forth whatever effort is necessary, and you count it a privilege to do so.

> Seek the Lord, and his strength: seek his face evermore.
> Psalms 105:4 KJV

The emphasis here is on continuity. Nothing is more painful than a temporary relationship. God is looking for some lasting friendships. Seeking the Lord is not a Sunday morning activity. It is a lifelong quest.

SEEKING GOD WILL REMAIN OUR PRIORITY, OUR PASSION AND OUR PURPOSE FOR EXISTENCE

Seeking God is something we are to do every day—in our homes, in our offices, in our schools, and in our stores. Seek His face always.

If we love Him, we will continually seek Him until we are, at last, in His ultimate presence in eternity. Even there, we will not stop seeking God. It will remain our priority, our passion, and our purpose for existence.

The ministry of seeking God will never end. It is a fundamental and ultimate priority. Seeking Him is what you will be doing in heaven forever. Offering Him your worship and adoration will be your only business. You will be fulfilling the first and greatest commandment; loving God with all your heart, soul, mind and strength.

Seeking God is so important that it could have easily been a drive or instinct built into the human being from creation. But God didn't want it that way. He wants the fellowship of caring and loving individuals, so He left you the option of not seeking His presence.

God doesn't want affection and adoration from a bunch of robots that praise and pray because they have to. When it is your decision to seek Him, it means something to God. It blesses Him and brings Him happiness.

MOTIVATION

Sometimes, the Israelites were motivated by fear or by the problems that invariably beset them when they turned from God. At other times, however, they were motivated by the many promises made in scripture to those who seek the Lord:

> The young lions do lack, and suffer hunger: but they
> that seek the Lord shall not want any good thing.
> Psalms 34:10 KJV

> And Judah gathered themselves together, to
> ask help of the Lord: even out of all the cities
> of Judah they came to seek the Lord.
> 2 Chronicles 20:4 KJV

BENEFITS

Seeking the Lord should be a consistent goal in life, for He is the source of everything that you need.

> Evil men understand not judgment: but they
> that seek the Lord understand all things.
> Proverbs 28:5 KJV

Tremendous understanding and revelation come to us when we seek the Lord. Answers can be found in His presence. He is the source of life and goodness.

> Seek the Lord, and ye shall live.
> Amos 5.6 KJV

Seeking the Lord effects your spiritual perception. It gives you an acute awareness of spiritual things. It opens us to a whole new world, one of which most of us are not even unaware.

Our Father in heaven wants those who willingly seek Him, not to seek Him out of obligation, or self-preservation, or any other reason. He wants those who choose to seek Him and worship Him because they love Him. He is their passion and their desire.

DANGER

Great majorities of people do not see their need for God. Many of them have more confidence in their own ability to work things out than they do in seeking the Lord for His direction. Their reliance is on something other than the Lord. They would rather take a shortcut and deal with things themselves. Perhaps it seems faster to them. They imagine that they will get quicker results.

TREMENDOUS UNDERSTANDING AND REVELATION COME TO US WHEN WE SEEK THE LORD

They are wrong. The prophet Isaiah warns us:

> Woe to those who go down to Egypt for help, who rely on horses, who trust in the multitude of their chariots and in the great strength of their horsemen, but do not look to the Holy One of Israel, or seek help from the Lord.
> Isaiah 31:1 NIV

King Rehoboam was not successful. The reason given by the Bible was that he did not prepare his heart to seek the Lord. He was not concerned about knowing the God of His forefathers.

> And he did evil, because he prepared not his heart to seek the Lord.
> 2 Chronicles 12:14 KJV

The Bible is full of other such sad accounts. Any man or woman who doesn't recognize his or her need for God is doomed to destruction.

ONE DAY

God's desire is not just for one nation to seek His presence. It is not just for one special group to come before Him. His desire is that all the nations seek His presence. His desire is that the whole world would come before

Him. Despite the rebellious nature of the nations, one day, according to biblical prophecy, the desire of God's heart will be fulfilled.

> And the inhabitants of one city shall go to another,
> saying, Let us go speedily to pray before the Lord, and
> to seek the Lord of hosts: I will go also. Yea, many
> people and strong nations shall come to seek the Lord
> of hosts in Jerusalem, and to pray before the Lord.
> Zechariah 8:21-22 KJV

Since the day Adam first sinned, God has had a plan to restore humanity back to Himself. He wants us to live in constant communion with Him. This is the message of the Gospel; this is the reason God sent His only Son into the world. He came to die for our sins so that we could be the friends of God once again.

We seek Him, however, not just for some benefit that might be derived from being in His presence, not to get answers to some problem we might have at the moment, not just to feel better. We seek Him because we love Him and we love to be near Him.

Some people only pray when they have a need. That is a selfish motive for seeking Him. We should seek God simply for Who He is, to be with Him, to fellowship with Him. Everything else will come. All the many other benefits will be yours.

Some Christians are asking, "What is in it for me?" They can be motivated to prayer and praise only if they are assured that they will get something out of it. If you are in fellowship with God only for what you can get out of it, you will not develop much of a relationship with Him.

We must ask ourselves am I seeking God's hand, or His face? Perhaps, then, we are looking for a handout, not a relationship. When you sit on God's lap, don't do it just to give Him your Christmas list. Do it to get to know Him better.

The cry of the Holy Spirit today is for His people to dedicate themselves to a serious quest for His manifest presence and to do it for all the right reasons.

God did this so that they would seek him
and perhaps reach out for him and find him,
though he is not far from any one of us.
Acts 17:27 NIV

THIRSTY

Do you have a burning desire to draw near to
God? Do you have a thirst for more of God? Do
you have a desire to be where He is? If so, you
are willing to pay any price necessary to quench
your thirst.

**WE MUST ASK
OURSELVES AM
I SEEKING GOD'S
HAND OR HIS FACE?**

God is not interested in half-hearted searching. He is calling for
intensity in our relationship. It brings Him pleasure to know that people
still exist who want to know Him so badly that they will do whatever is
necessary to fulfill that longing.

Seek the Lord and his strength, seek his face continually.
1 Chronicles 16:11 KJV

You can experience His presence here now. He is waiting for you to
pursue Him. The promise is that God-chasers will be God-finders.

...break up your fallow ground: for it is time to seek the
Lord, till he come and rain righteousness upon you.
Hosea 10:12 NIV

Then you will call upon me and come and
pray to me, and I will hear you.
Jeremiah 29:12 ESV

You must take the initiative and cry out, out loud. It is not something
you do in your head but with your voice. Then come to God. That means
to move toward, go after Him in worship and pursue Him. These are the
conditions to seeking God.

Then, Jeremiah says, pray. That is to intervene, interpose, intercede, or supplicate to Him and He will listen, attend with interest and give heed to hear, answer, and grant your request.

> You will seek me and find me, when
> you seek me with all your heart.
> Jeremiah 29:13 ESV

The promise continues. When you require, desire, or request to seek to find, to seek to secure, or to seek the face of God it is for a purpose. It is to find Him—to secure, acquire, receive, meet, discover, and encounter God.

He is a rewarder of those that diligently seek Him with all their heart. When you search, require, and enquire of God with every part of your heart He is the award. He rewards you with Himself. What a joy! What a discovery!

CHAPTER TWENTY-NINE
STUDY GUIDE

SCRIPTURE

Read Hosea 10 and Micah 4.

QUESTIONS

1. What has always been God's plan for humanity?

2. What does it take to seek God's presence?

3. What does it mean to seek God?

4. Why doesn't God make all humans seek Him?

5. How can we encounter God's manifest presence?

6. What does God promise us if we seek Him?

REFLECTION

1. Do you remember a time when you were the most passionate about pursuing God's manifest presence?

2. What does it mean to you to seek God?

3. What is the Holy Spirit saying to you through this chapter?

PRAYER / CONFESSION

Heavenly Father,

Increase in me a greater desire to know your manifest presence. I want to constantly seek You wherever I am.

Holy Spirit put a passion in my heart to seek God's presence that I may search for Him until I find the satisfaction of knowing Him.

In Jesus Name,

Amen

MEDITATE / MEMORIZE

You will seek me and find me, when
you seek me with all your heart.
Jeremiah 29:13 ESV

30

CHAPTER THIRTY
CHALLENGE

○———————————————————————————————○

We have come to the end of our journey. There remains one question: Do you want to have the desire to encounter God? You can experience God's revealed presence up close and personal.

What kind of passion do you have for the Lord's presence?

> As the heart pants and longs for the water brooks so I pant and long for You, O God. My inner self thirsts for God, for the living God. When shall I come and behold the face of God? My tears have been my food day and night, while men say to me all the day long, where is your God?
> Psalms 42:1–3 AMP

When was the last time you were really thirsty for the Lord's presence? Was it in church one Sunday last year when you went to the altar to let God know you were serious about Him? Was it at youth camp ten years ago? Or has it been even longer?

How about now? Are you thirsty for God's presence right now? Do you long to live in His presence and walk in His presence? How would that desire rank among your top five priorities in life?

PRIORITY

David said:

> One thing have I asked of the Lord, that will I seek after,
> inquire for and [insistently] require, that I may dwell in
> the house of the Lord [in His presence] all the days of
> my life, to behold and gaze upon the beauty [the sweet
> attractiveness and the delightful loveliness] of the Lord.
> Psalms 27:4 AMP

Do you feel distant from God? Do you sense a separation between His presence and yourself? Have you withdrawn yourself from Him for some reason? Or do you even feel totally cut off from the Lord, removed, severed, and far away from His presence?

If so, are you satisfied to stay that way? Are you satisfied to live in that state? Today the Lord is drawing you close to Him.

> You have said, seek My face—inquire for and require My
> presence [as your vital need]. My heart says to You Your
> face [Your presence], Lord will I seek, inquire for and
> require [of necessity and on the authority of Your Word].
> Hide not Your face from me; turn not Your servant away
> in anger, You have been my help! Cast me not off.
> Psalms 27:8–9 AMP

YOUR MOVE

There is no need to feel distant from the Lord anymore. He has made it clear in His Word that His desire is for you to live in His manifest presence. Father has provided a way for you to come into His presence and to get close to Him. And He has shown you the methods of approaching

Him anytime, anywhere. He is calling you now. Come close to God, and He will come close to you.

> Come close to God, and God will come close to you...
> James 4:8 NLT

It is your move. God has done everything possible to ensure your fellowship with Him. Now, He awaits your decision. He is anxiously watching to see if you will come to Him. Don't disappoint Him.

FATHER HAS PROVIDED A WAY FOR YOU TO COME INTO HIS PRESENCE AND TO GET CLOSE TO HIM

STEPS

Take that first step now. I challenge you to begin right now to develop a passion for the manifest presence of the Lord. Let His presence be your highest request and your greatest need. And may all other things become secondary in your life.

If you want more of this infatuation for God's presence, you can acquire it. It is not out of your reach and available to all believers.

Here are some steps you can follow:

1. Develop a Devotional Time with the Lord. Begin a diligent and consistent personal worship time with Him. Schedule it and keep your appointment.

2. Shut the Door. This may seem silly but it is not. This is the first principle Jesus taught about prayer. "When you pray, go into your room, and when you have shut your door, pray to your Father who is in the secret place." (Matthew 6:6 KJV) To get into God's presence you should shut the door to everything else. Shut yourself in with your Father who is in the secluded place. He is there waiting. All you have to do is get in with Him and close the door.

3. Start by Singing Praise to Jesus. Remember, God manifests His presence when His children sing spontaneously to Him. Sing your extemporaneous praise and prayers to God out loud.

4. Play Worship Music. Sometimes we all need help. Ana Paula Valadão enjoys playing anointed worship songs in the background as she sings her prayers and praise to God. Playing worship music creates an atmosphere and a heart posture of worship. It also gives you music to sing to.

5. Read His Word Expressively. Ana Paula Valadão highly recommends you open the Bible and read God's word as if He is speaking directly to you. Reading God's thoughts helps you know Him better and develop a deeper relationship with Him. Read the Bible out loud for a while. Hearing your own words will build your faith because faith comes by hearing the Word of God. This will enable you to develop confidence in hearing your voice and increase your appetite for His manifest presence.

WAIT IN HIS PRESENCE, LISTENING TO HIM

6. Take Your Time. Don't rush, but take time to focus on Him and to fully express your desires to Him. Wait in His presence, listening to Him. As you get to know Him, your love for Him will grow. Before long, you will have a greater passion for more of His presence. You don't have anything more important to do. Allow a God-consciousness to slowly seep into your soul. After a while you will look forward to these times alone with the Lord, as David did.

7. Fast a Meal. Deny your flesh and its appetites and let your soul know that your spirit is in charge. Your spiritual passion needs to dominate over your flesh if you want to have more power to press in to encounter the manifest presence of God.

COMMITMENT

If this is your desire, I want to lead you in prayer. Please pray with me as you read these words. Say them with passion from your heart and if you can say them outloud.

Gracious Heavenly Father,

I have made my decision to draw near to You in worship and to seek Your presence because I want to know You better.

Deliver me from seeking an "experience." Help me to seek Your face and to develop a hunger for Your presence. Let Your nearness in my life be my most earnest affection.

Forgive me for having other desires or putting other things before You. Cleanse my spirit of lethargy and indifference. Deliver me from the routine of worship, from business as usual, from form without force and liturgy without life.

May Your Holy Spirit energize the new creation that is in me to worship You in spirit and in reality. Make my worship whole-hearted, warm, and vibrant. Remind me, whenever necessary, that the portal of praise is always open for me to come into Your revealed presence.

I make You my quest and my infatuation. You are my love and my life. To You I give all my affection and adoration today and always.

In the name of Jesus,

Amen

CHAPTER THIRTY
STUDY GUIDE

SCRIPTURE

Read Read Psalms 27.

QUESTIONS

1. What was the "one thing" David asked God for?

2. How would you define a passion for God's presence?

3. What was David's response to God instructing him to seek His face?

4. What is the face of God?

5. In James 4, when does it say God will come close to us?

6. What are the seven steps of pursuing the presence of God?

REFLECTION

1. Was there a time when you burned with passion for God?

2. What will you do different after reading this chapter?

3. What is the Holy Spirit saying to you through this chapter?

PRAYER / CONFESSION

Heavenly Father,

I realize that there is only one thing that is essential in my life. So, I receive the challenge to passionately pursue your manifest presence.

Holy Spirit put it in my mind and spirit to do the spiritual disciplines necessary to experience and enjoy God's manifest presence. I desire to know Him, walk and talk with Him as my new lifestyle.

I pray this in Jesus Name,

Amen

MEDITATE / MEMORIZE

> One thing have I asked of the Lord, that will I seek after, inquire for and [insistently] require, that I may dwell in the house of the Lord [in His presence] all the days of my life, to behold and gaze upon the beauty [the sweet attractiveness and the delightful loveliness] of the Lord.
> Psalms 27:4 AMP

LAMAR BOSCHMAN

A sought after speaker and mentor, LaMar Boschman is a pioneer and a father of the worship we enjoy today. He is known for equipping others in transcendent worship and the manifest presence of God. Here is a snapshot of LaMar in his own words:

From the day my father bought me my first guitar at fourteen years old, I remember the joy I experienced in writing and singing songs. At sixteen, two friends and I recorded our first album and it was during that time that I began to sense God's presence when I sang to Him. After moving to Vancouver, British Columbia, I became part of a musically

progressive church and discovered what praise and the presence of God was. Upon finishing Bible college there, God launched me into full-time itinerant ministry—my life would never be the same.

From the age of 22, I became one of the first itinerant worship ministries traveling the world leading worship and teaching about praise and worship and the presence of God. Looking back when few of us who created the first worship seminars in the United States, pioneered the concept of worship leading and worship teams. Over the years I have hosted Worship Institutes and Weekend Encounters to equip leaders in many places of the world.

Today I still speak at conferences and churches, teach at university and colleges, blog, write books, and mentor younger leaders. I live in Texas with my wife and we are members of Gateway Church (www.gatewaypeople.com).

WHAT OTHERS SAY

For four decades, LaMar Boschman has helped people connect with the presence of God. He has been one of the pioneers and fathers of contemporary worship. As the author of numerous books and videos, LaMar Boschman's teaching and worship leading has impacted churches and leaders around the world. The gift he carries has changed church cultures and redefined the paths of many church leaders.

"LaMar Boschman has a gift to help people understand the importance of worship! I was impressed with his heart for God and his heart to help people encounter God." — **ROBERT MORRIS**

OTHER RESOURCES by LaMar Boschman

AUTHENTIC · Exploring the Mysteries of Real Worship: When most Christians hear the word worship, they automatically associate it with singing a song. However, real worship is more about your relationship with the great God of heaven and earth. This book contains a study guide and is perfect for small group study of worship.

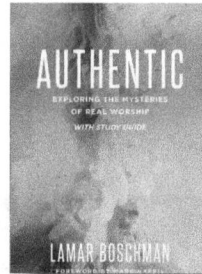

A HEART OF WORSHIP · Experience a Rebirth of Worship. This book will energize and invigorate your worship life, changing forever the way   you veiw your ability and call to worship. It is used as a text book in universities and colleges. It is perfect for small group study with family, team or school.

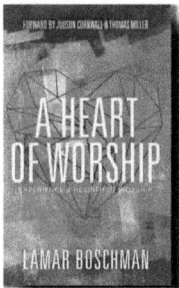

CONNECT WITH LAMAR

LAMARBOSCHMAN.COM

- BLOG - Subscribe and gain fresh revelation on spiritual principles that will empower your life and ministry.

- RESOURCES - Discover books and audio downloads from LaMar.

- PODCAST - The Music of God

- SCHEDULE - Invite LaMar to speak at your event.

SOCIAL MEDIA

- YOUTUBE - Find new teaching video series from LaMar

- SOCIAL MEDIA - Follow LaMar on Instagram, Google+, Facebook, and Twitter!

www.ingramcontent.com/pod-product-compliance
Lightning Source LLC
LaVergne TN
LVHW051456080426
835509LV00017B/1779